UNIVERSITY
WITHDRAWN FROM THE LIBRARY
University of Nottingham
DEPARTMENT OF CONTINUING EDUCATION
LIBRARY
14-22 Shakespeare Street, Nottingham, NG1 4FQ
Tel: 0115 951 6510
Acc. No. 31730a Class No. 301.42
O/S
N7760.
.L2

John Lash

The Hero

Manhood and Power

With 132 illustrations, 16 in colour

Thames and Hudson

On the cover. Front: Diego Rivera, *Agrarian leader Zapata*, fresco, 1931. Back: detail from *The Sage Shakadeva instructing King Savikshit*, c. 1760

Any copy of this book issued by the publisher as a paperback is sold subject to the condition that it shall not by way of trade or otherwise be lent, resold, hired out or otherwise circulated without the publisher's prior consent in any form of binding or cover other than that in which it is published and without a similar condition including these words being imposed on a subsequent purchaser.

© 1995 Thames and Hudson Ltd, London

All Rights Reserved. No part of this publication may be reproduced or transmitted in any form or by any means, electronic or mechanical, including photocopy, recording or any other information storage and retrieval system, withour prior permission in writing from the publisher.

British Library Cataloguing-in-Publication Data
A catalogue record for this book is available from the British Library

ISBN 0-500-81047-8

Printed and bound in Singapore by C.S. Graphics

Contents

The Hero

Origins of the Hero 5
From Hunter to Warrior 12
For Mortal to Aid Mortal 16
Tragedy and Transfiguration 21
The Ever-changing Quest 27

Plates 33

Themes 65

Sunmen and Phallic Cults 66
Serpent Power, Dragon Treasure 68
Initiation and Ordeal 70
Herakles and the Royal Lion 72
The Wild Hunt 74
Hero and Horse 76
Arms and the Man 78
Minotauromachia 80
The Hero in Love 82
The Hero Facing Death 84
Woman as Hero 86
Ancestral and National Heroes 88
War Heroes through the Ages 90
The Hero Facing Adversity 92
Temptations of the Hero 94

Further Reading 96

Acknowledgments 96

The shaman exemplifies two main aggressive traits of the prehistoric hero: man's skill as a hunter, combined with the ability to venture mystically into other worlds. (Pottery figure of a shaman, late Chou or early Han Dynasty.)

Origins of the Hero

Myth and history preserve the names of many men regarded as heroes, an abundance of figures who seem to have attained a superhuman stature. Almost anyone can act heroically – for instance, a mother who rescues her children from a fire – but the hero embodies something more. He possesses a consistent capacity for action that surpasses the norm of man or woman. This contrast between what may be heroic in action and what identifies a hero in the purest sense of the term, is essential. Both morally and physically, the hero is nevertheless *of* the human species, not superior to it, not beyond it. Even if his earliest prototypes are partially divine, the hero is, in his prime, fully human rather than superhuman. A rare configuration of traits and a striking style of action mark him as having *arete*, excellence. In excelling and exceeding himself, the hero becomes a model of higher potential for his clan, his race or nation, even for humanity at large.

Foremost in the heroic configuration is virility, the essence of the masculine sex. The hero is undeniably *he*, the male of the human species. Gender is an issue here, for ideally the hero incarnates masculinity in its best, most noble aspects, even though he is potentially equal to the worst of which his sex is capable. His career is turbulent and controversial because virility is close kin to violence – perhaps even its dark, unruly twin. In all cultures, the hero is uniquely charged with the responsibility to use violent force, as the situation requires, without being consumed by it. Originally, the violence perpetrated by men was imbued with both sacred and survival value. Changes in the value ascribed to violent force account in large measure for successive shifts in the role of the hero through the ages.

While the hero cannot be considered without some significant sidelong glances at heroines, these cannot be taken as his cross-sexual parallels or counterparts. The hero has no exact counterpart in the opposite sex, and heroines who act in the manner of the hero are wild anomalies in world mythology and racial lore: the fabled Amazons, Athene, the armored war-goddess of Greece, Joan of Arc, the virgin in full knight's regalia; also Boadicea and the ferocious warrior-women celebrated among the Celts. These exceptions prove the rule that heroic identity and masculine prowess are based on the mastery of certain interior (i.e., 'feminine') powers of the body, predominantly but not exclusively exploited by men.

Universal evidence of the heroic quest reveals a threefold structure: the 'eternal triangle' of hero-monster-woman. For instance, in Polynesia, Maui-tikititi-a-Ataraga, Wonderworker, the Timid, Begotten of Ascending Shadow, fights the phallic monster eel, Te Tuna, for the luscious maiden, Hina. Their combat involves a test-ordeal where each one slips like a virus into the body of the other, disappears completely, and attacks it from within. The same plot is tirelessly repeated in European tales of chivalry where a knight in shining armour fights a dragon for a lady, but these later, less 'primitive' versions of the heroic contest rarely show so vividly how hero and adversary are corporeally interfused. In some renditions, adapted to a patriarchal ethos which opposes the hero to the feminine element, the monster and the woman are interfused. This is patently false, although the relationship between hero and woman does become more and more troubling and ambivalent as the quest changes and evolves down through the ages.

Masculine surfeit of life-force is emblematically captured in the multiple heads of this funerary statue, representing the 'mana' or magical force of several departed heroes. (Wooden figure from Vanua Lava, Banks Islands, Melanesia.)

The sage and the saint, or saviour, commonly treated as variants of the hero, are really deviants from his pure and primary expression. A third variant, the warrior, remains close to his essence. These three primary masculine types – sage, saviour and warrior-hero – arise from different origins and reflect conflicting ideologies of power. Deeply implicated in problems of power, the hero in his true calling never uses it to dominate others. Heroes fight their equals, other heroes, or take on monstrous adversaries, but to challenge or overpower ordinary people is beneath them. The mission of the hero in all his variants consists not merely in the management of force, but in the mastery of *an excess of force*. His challenge is to face forces gone out of control, exceeding their proper limits, and he himself embodies the dangerous superfluity of such forces.

By contrast, the sage or saint embodies the equilibrium achieved by perfecting resources common to us all, inner powers of mind and spirit. He is the idealization of the human norm, while the hero is supranormal. Even under harrowing attacks by demons, the saint will repel or refuse excessive displays of power in favour of centring himself in the still, calm infinity within the soul. He is peace and perfection, while the hero is violence, excess and all-too-human fallibility. Rare examples of hero-saints who blend pacific and aggressive traits occur in Indo-Tibetan lore: for instance, Saraha and Naropa, polished versions of Bon Po shamans. The legend of Saint Francis describes his attraction to the violence and glamour of chivalry before his conversion.

The third masculine type, the saviour, epitomizes the power to perform cosmic acts of redemption or compensation, a motif quite alien to the calling of the hero. At first this contrast may seem unlikely, for the hero is so often pictured as intervening in a desperate situation. From Perseus freeing Andromeda to medieval knights rescuing damsels in distress to Indiana Jones delivering his ex-girlfriend from the Nazis, the hero is always saving someone or something. Yes, but rescue is not redemption. To redeem means to make up for what has been lost or harmed, even restore it to its original state. The redeemer who acts to preserve cosmic law and eternal justice will often mete out punishment to those responsible for disrupting it, as Christ does in the Last Judgment; but the hero never performs in this way, assured that his actions are supported and sanctified by a higher order. He does not restore what has been lost: he protects and preserves what is at risk of being lost. He retaliates if honour is threatened, but he does not redress on principle. He displays autonomy, not authority.

The distinction is crucial because the entire complex of redemptive theology in the West, derived from the saviour mythos of Indo-Iranian dualism, distracts and detracts from the true ancestry of the hero. His origins lie elsewhere, deep in prehistory, in the unwritten survival-dramas of the species and in the ethics and practices of polytheistic nature-cults whose traces lie piled like rubble at the base of those looming monuments, the Indo-European mythologies. His roots have been overlaid by vast rescripting of source materials from aboriginal cultures, oral traditions, and the dramatic-mimetic arts. Often cast as star player in theocratic and authoritarian texts, the hero remains true to his origins outside fundamentalist belief-systems. Even when he appears to act like a redeemer-figure, he never relies on a transcendental framework of values to justify and support his action.

St George killing the Dragon is the most well-known of countless stories in which a hero overcomes a monster to rescue a maiden. The three-point motif, universal in cultural mythology, precedes the religious ideology of redemption that later comes to be attached to it. (Miniature from an Ethiopian manuscript, 17th century.)

In Hindu myth, Vishnu is the original type of the saviour, the divinity who descends to save the world by incarnating in a sequence of ten avatars. This Indo-Persian motif of salvation from on high recurs in the drama of the Christian messiah and certainly seems to inform the heroic mission, but for every Saint George there was a pre-Christian hero who has been re-scripted to fit the role of redeemer. The question remains, What were the character and motives of the hero before his adaptation?

Vishnu belongs to the pantheon of Aryan gods, but preceding the Aryan invasions (variously dated from 1400 BC to 4400 BC) India was permeated by the Dravidian culture, especially in the south. The Dasyus, or dark ones, who populated the subcontinent were probably of a Melanesian race surviving today (just barely) among the aborigines of Australia. Their supreme deity was Shiva, the pre-Aryan god who truly prefigures the hero. He is an ecstatic forest-dweller, a hunter and warrior as well as an ascetic who masters the powers hidden in his own body. No transcorporeal and upperworld redeemer like Vishnu, he is a denizen of the underworld, whose allies are snakes and ravening beasts. He is called *Pasupathi*, Lord of the Animals, for his mastery of hunting skills and survival strategies. He reveres the life-force yet he also kills, mystically incorporating the bestial strength of the prey. Like shamans worldwide, he works with an *excess* of forces, magical and sexual, the surfeit of wild, superabundant, overflowing nature contained in his psychosomatic structure. He is supervitality in peak form, fully human in his resources though said to be 'god-like' because of his excessive exploitation of them.

The *Rig-Veda*, sacred book of the Aryans, denounces the orgiastic cults of Shiva where the body of woman and the male phallus alike were revered as instruments of sacred potency, but it was from such rude cultic origins that the hero was born. According to Manu, the Hindu-Aryan law-giver, the people of Dravida were originally *Kshatriya*, of the warrior caste, but they sank to the lower caste of *Sudra*, servants, because they did not observe the sacred rites of the Vedas. This is a white-washed version of how the Aryan invaders repressed and absorbed the native culture of southern India. Nevertheless, it gives away the clue that the Dravidians were 'warriors' similar to the kind now understood to have descended from the hunter cultures of the Lower Paleolithic in Europe. The transition from hunter to warrior (described at more length in the following chapter) marks the initial emergence of the hero upon the world stage. Far from being a champion of the celestial gods, he is a 'wild man' from the hinterlands. All his superior gifts, the marks of his *arete*, both physical and moral, are refinements of our savage, instinctual endowment, the survival wisdom of *homo sapiens*.

Shiva's equivalent in Greco-Latin myth is Dionysos, the raving, charismatic god notorious for his *mania*, the excess of ecstatic-destructive vitality emanated by his mere presence. The source of Dionysian excess is the body, loaded with the occult potencies of its physio-chemical structure, still largely mysterious to us today, yet exploited to astounding excess in feats of Indian yoga and rigours of heroic initiation. Furious, superheated force is the male equivalent to the procreative largesse of the female, pictured in the voluptuous overmodelling of Stone Age goddess icons from Laussel and Willendorf. Superfluity of the 'solar-phallic' type, demonstrated in the figure and feats of the warrior-hero, is variously called *furor, wut, lust, kudos, ferg, fury*. Rage is the male complement to nurture, and equally essential to the survival of the species. The pure potency of benign aggression, it persists as a survival tool and an heroic virtue for millenia before it degenerates into the pathological blood-lust of the Mongol invasions, the Jehad and the Crusades, Aztec war-games, the Stalinist purges, and kamikazi bombing missions.

Divorced from its proper moral code, the heroic ideal of excess power becomes perverted into extreme forms of aggression, such as the Japanese kamikazi mission in which pilots, full of ideological zeal and worked up into a suicidal rage, deliberately crash their bomb-laden planes into their targets. (Suzuki Mitsuru: *Graduating students depart for the Front.*)

As Shiva stands apart from the Vedic-Brahmanic cult of patriarchal dominance, Dionysos too is an outsider, feared and rejected by those who hold to the clear rule of Apollonian rationality. His origins are obscure, but it is certain that the rapturous communion with savage nature which he represents was common to the pre-Hellenic peoples, the Pelasgians who inhabited the wilds of the Peloponessus, haunts of Pan and the satyrs. Late Greek legend tells of a journey of Dionysos to India, linking him to his Hindu twin. He and Shiva both have the bull as their double; both go naked, are intimate with wild animals, celebrate orgiastic pleasure and willing surrender to death. All these attributes, derived from the hunting cultures of the Paleolithic Age spanning back to 650,000 BC, are revived and reenacted in the character and actions of the hero. Archaic traces always show when the hero is present, neither deviated from his origins nor adapted to alien causes.

For instance, in Celtic legend we find the clan hero, Fergus mac Roich, whose name comes from *ferg*, the superheated rage of the hunter-warrior. His full name, 'Fergus son of the great horse,' refers dually to sexual prowess and his totemic identification with the solar horse, common in heroic lore. His consort is the warrior-woman, Queen Mebd (Maev), 'Drunk Woman', a tantrika of boundless erotic drive. Celtic warriors (the male ones, at least) frequently went into battle stark naked with an excess of vital forces literally streaming from every pore. Cuchulainn, another Celtic folk-hero, slays a hundred foes in a night, repels fourteen javelins at a stroke, runs raster than the wind. Exaggeration, comic and hideous by turns, is a trope found in all accounts of the hero. Both the action of the hero and the language used to describe it exhibit the motif of superfluity, power in excess, male surfeit.

Shiva and Dionysos are clearly gods, divine predecessors of the hero who is purely, essentially human. The same line of descent occurs in other superhuman figures as diverse as Maui in Polynesia, Shen Nung in China, Odin in Scandinavia, or any number of trickster-heroes from the American west. All these are quasi-gods of dubious parentage. In the broad sense they are indeed hero types, but in the narrow sense (considered here) they merely prefigure the true identity of the hero who is a man and mortal. Specific instances of heroes who partake of divinity (noted below) are rare. Among the Eskimos and the jungle-dwelling tribes of South America alike, he is viewed as exclusively human. Deification of a hero, as occurs with the Greek Herakles and the Japanese Yamato-dake, always indicates the deliberate reworking of popular materials to fit a racial or authoritarian agenda.

The same applies for 'sacralized' heroes such as Ezra in the Old Testament. For the Hebrews the hero was an outsider, an exile or marginal figure who raises a voice of moral outrage against the corrupt or impotent authority of the priesthood. Remaining a loner and a law unto himself, he was true to the heroic mould, but when hero-types such as Enoch, Moses, Jared and Elijah are shown to draw their strength and inspiration from an extrahuman source of power, and present themselves as its sovereign instrument, another system of values has been imposed. Both the Aryan and Abrahamic ideologies of power abound with heroes enlisted to serve a higher power, but these scripts dehumanize the hero and distract us from empathic identification with his lonely and often desperate path. Ironically, male-biased revisions of the heroic quest are the ones that most seriously impede our view of the genuine motives that work and weave in the heart of the hero.

An oystercatcher presented with an oversize egg of another species will respond to this 'supernormal stimulation' by attempting to hatch it, exactly as the hero responds to the challenge of taking on overwhelming forces – and thereby, if he succeeds, attaining a 'peak experience' that strengthens the survival power of his species.

Among the Church fathers, *dei gentium* was the derogatory term for pagan and classical heroes like Aeneas and Odysseus: the gods of the countryfolk, the heathen, the pagans. To put it without Christian bias, heroes were as good as gods for those who did not believe in *the* God, the One and Only. In antiquity the hero cults were centres of deep civic piety and humanistic feeling where the people found inspiration to strive toward noble and generous action, not to be rewarded for it by the betterment of their souls, but simply because that is the best, and the least, any human being can do. In the pagan ethos, the hero was never mistaken for a god in disguise. It was not a superhuman divinity he embodies, but human dignity. Morally, he is the epitome of that higher striving later celebrated to excess by the Romantics, known in anthropology as 'supernormal sign stimulus' and in humanistic psychology as the capacity for 'peak experience'. Heroic discipline requires access to a surfeit of power or strategic skill, and the prudence to regulate its use. In classical idiom, these are *fortitudo* and *sapientia*, Latin words used by Virgil to describe the Homeric virtues of the Trojan hero, Aeneas.

We may well ask, What is specifically 'masculine' about this attainment of moral-physical superiority? Are not women also capable of peak expression of our species' potential? Certainly, but the hero in his trials and triumphs displays exclusively one dimension of our common endowment: *the full ripening of the aggressive instinct which assures survival by the mastery of overwhelming forces rather than by adaptation to them*, adaptation being the forte of the female. Hence the hero is typically a monster-slayer whose powers are equal to nature itself. As a mythic image, he carries the phylogenetic memory of the Paleoanthropic hunter facing the dangers of the wild, contending with beasts of prey who originally served him both as a source of nourishment and a sacrament in the original rites of mystic communion.

Although he epitomizes the male gender, the hero in all his variants is profoundly bound to the opposite sex. At the cultic origins, it is Woman who situates the hero in the world at large. Typically he depends upon the refuge provided by a matriarchal society, or goddess-based culture. Odin drew his magical shamanic powers from the cauldron of inspiration protected by the daughter of the titan, Suttung. Among the Blackfoot of Montana, Kut-o-yis ('Blood Clot'), is assisted in developing his excess of powers by an old nanny. In the legend of White Youth told among the Yakut shamans of Siberia, the hero, finding himself alone in a milk-white vastness, appeals to the High Mistress embodied in a sacred tree. The goddess sends a milky rain that transforms the tree she inhabits into a woman who suckles and protects the young hero. In the far west, trickster-heroes such as Momoya of the Chumash (California Coast) grow up under the tutelage of a powerful woman known simply as the grandmother (ie. Great Mother). Herakles, too, is fatefully and ambivalently bound to womankind. His name means 'Glory of Hera', she the Olympian mother-goddess who drives him to excel, to exceed himself. He, the ultimate model of 'man-power' in Greco-Latin myth, dresses as a woman in the manner of Siberian shamans and even at times acts as menial servant to various women, such as Omphale. (Moral: even a hero can do the dishes on occasion.)

From his first appearance the hero is neither a product nor an exponent of the patriarchal order. Instead, heroes consistently originate in those great preliterate mother cultures whose traces are found at Mohenjo Daro and Harappa in India, Catal Huyuk in Anatolia, Malta, Minoan Crete, Old Europe (the Balkans), the Magdalenian matrix of Southern France, and Ireland before Christianity. The cultic and cultural origins of the hero in matriarchy support recent psychological theories which stress the crucial role of the mother, or mother-figure, in the early formation of the masculine character.

Enlisting the hero as a model for *machismo* and an apologist for male dominance is therefore utterly wrong, but the error persists due to a long history of misrepresentation. In a close study, the hero has to be set apart from the patriarchal protagonist, better designated as the 'champion', the man who upholds the establishment and fights for abstract causes at the expense of flesh-and-blood values. This crucial distinction runs far back through the mythic lore where hero and champion are often depicted in the same text. The *Epic of Gilgamesh*, for instance, is one of the formative hero-tales of the West. It presents Gilgamesh as the triumphant regent of Ur, a champion of civilization but also a tyrant who flaunts his power by taking any woman he fancies. Offended at his license, the people beg the high gods for a rival and so Enkidu, a wild creature, is fashioned from mud: for the cause of violated women this hero is created. When they wrestle and find their strength matched, a bond develops between Gilgamesh and Enkidu, champion and hero. After living in the wild with animals who treat him as a friend, Enkidu is lured into human society by the charms of a temple courtesan: that is, he confronts his own interiority through the feminine and becomes initiated into the path of personal engagement with the Other. His friendship with Gilgamesh is troubled because the champion follows one code of rules, insuring him mundane prestige and power over others, while Enkidu, as we say, 'cannot adapt'. Eventually he is cursed by Ishtar, i.e., overwhelmed by (his own) interiority and the intersubjective demands posed by the Other. His death traumatizes Gilgamesh with a terrible sense of loss. Enkidu is authentic and dies heroically for it. Gilgamesh goes on to search for solace in immortality, in the Beyond, unable to take the here-and-now as all there is; but the grief of the pseudo-heroic champion for the suffering of the defiant hero is a potent motif that will recur countless times in Western myth and literature.

Thus, the champion and his variants, the racist idol and demagogue, stand as far apart from the pure and central figure of the hero as do the sacralized moralist, saint and saviour. The hero is never power-mongering, sanctimonious or self-righteous, although he is prey to arrogance, abuse and flawed judgment. He confronts situations, he does not embrace causes. If he takes sides at all, it is for challenge of the occasion, not for ideological reasons. His code of power, rooted in moral independence and dignified acceptance of the suffering it entails, continues to sustain us when other creeds, especially the transcendent ideologies of sin and obligation, fail to square against the brute facts of life. He redirects us continually to the Sacred as it can be found in vitality and the power of choice, not in the Beyond or its promises. The hero rejects transcendence for *amor fati*, love of the act for its own sake, whatever its consequences. True to his origins, he represents the wisdom of our precious natural endowment, the innate and mysterious resources of our *somatic* organization, imbued with instincts learned and refined through millennia of trial and error, risk and triumph, rescue and perdition.

From Hunter to Warrior

Heroism began when the male of the species made his first attempts to encounter and master powers in nature far exceeding his own. Simply and literally, the Sacred is powerful: from the Sanskrit verb-root *sak-*, 'to be potent, full of power'. The earth is sacred because its power sustains us, far surpassing ours yet in some instances calling upon us to match it, lest we perish. To this call man responded in his first adventures as the hero, exploits undertaken at the beginning of an unwritten, prehistoric narrative that reaches us, full of emotive impact, through a stretch of half a million years, conservatively speaking. Anthropology teaches that man has passed the first 95% of his experience as a hunter. From monster-slayers like Beowulf, Maui, Sigurd and Theseus right down to Superman and James Bond, all the celebrated guises of the hero share as their common ancestor that unnamed, unsung figure crudely remembered as the 'caveman'.

Mastering power by taking it to excess, the hero brought man to his own sense of engaging the sacred. As surely as woman was revered for fecundating powers embodied in her yet beyond her control, man was venerated for his virility independent of its procreative aspect. The swelling of a woman's body in pregnancy is a momentous feat of nature that requires no exertion on her part. Both in her external form and her hidden internal organs, woman is designed to reproduce the species, and she does so with brutal exaction, under compulsion of a higher order. No wonder woman has perennially been viewed as pure and selfless instrument of nature, an honour entailing the risk that she will be overwhelmed and enslaved by her own biological functions.

By contrast, masculinity is only revealed in the superfluity man achieves by voluntary exertion. Nature leaves the male free to discover in himself the equivalent to that dimension of prodigious power openly demonstrated in woman's ordeal of gestation and birth. Between the sexes there exists therefore an intrinsic and inescapable competition in which man is the dark horse. Darwin observed that the female tends to preserve and lead back to the norm of any species, while the male exhibits a wider range of physio-anatomical variation and an excess of display. Modern studies of embryonic development confirm how the higher degree of masculine self-definition is claimed by arduous disengagement from a female 'ground-plan'. Likewise, man realizes himself as hero, not merely by efforts, but by an excess and exaggeration of efforts.

Prehistoric rock carvings show solar and phallic markings in the form of rays or antler-like emanations to describe the surfeit of vital power manifested somatically by the hero. (Bronze Age petroglyphs in the Camonica Valley, Italy.)

Consequently, the role of hyperbole in heroic exploits is prominent. Killer-of-Enemies, a hero of the Jicarilla Apaches, boasts the extent of his powers, claiming that his body and his word are as large as the world itself. He is 'larger than life', and his physical acts are equal to acts of nature. Even the seasons, attesting to the comfort and regularity of the Feminine, are no more formidable than his words, his efforts, his devotions. Both the underworld and the sky are contained in his body: i.e., morphologically reproduced in his psychosomatic structure.

In cosmologies based on somatic values, woman's body was typically equated to nature, the earth itself, while man's body was equated to the cosmos entire. In ancient India, the tasks required to raise the cosmic powers inherent in man and demonstrate through him, by voluntary effort, what nature demonstrates spontaneously in woman, were called *tapas*, 'ascesis, austerity, exertion'. The first rishis and yogis were renowned for their superior feats of bodily discipline. *Tapas*, the basis of all surviving forms of yoga, induced a hypertrophy of the internal body-functions, often by suppressing them. Its aim was to raise metabolic heat to an excessive, unnatural degree. In shamanism, a matrix of vast heroic lore, its effects were often amplified by the ingestion of sacred plants and potions, such as soma. These practices probably evolved through a formal, organizational phase as early as 6000 BC, and they continue to this day in the Tibetan ordeal of tummo, 'heat-yoga' so intense that the monk with his naked body dries blanket after blanket that has been soaked in an icy mountain torrent. Likewise, in the Irish epic, *The Cattle Raid of Cooley*, the warriors of Ulster radiate a heat so strong they melt the snow to thirty paces in all directions. The use of heat in the 'vision quest' and heroic rites of passage persists today in the sweat-lodges of the American West.

But for millennia before that remote time when man, aspiring to spiritual heights, cultivated the mystic heat, the hero had already encountered its awesome power arising within himself, spontaneously, time and time again, through dangerous and exhilarating exertions of another kind – the perils of the hunt.

Man is born of woman, but the hero is born of the hunt. Imagine the atmosphere at the scene of a motorway pileup, but charged with a festive air, even moments of jocularity, and strangely interfused with modulations of deep religious solemnity: such was the mood of the hunt. Here was the first heroic combat, a contest with animals many times more powerful than man, and, at the same time, a sacred rite of transubstantiation, the exchange of life for life. Hunter-hero and prey were bound in kinship and reverence. To kill was to adore, to worship the infinite transmutability of the lifeforce and partake of its bounty. This mystic participation with life in all its savage beauty bestowed upon the Stone Age hero a sense of reverence not referred in any way to a remote transcendental realm beyond the senses.

Arthurian knights who battle elusive phantoms and fire-breathing dragons, Herakles wrestling with the Hydra, Odysseus outsmarting the Cyclops, Hunaphu of the Quiche Maya who stalks the scorpion double of the sorcerer Seven Macaw, No-Cha the Taoist wild boy who boils the Eastern Sea when he enters it, Tinirau the Maori chieftain who avenges the death of his magical whale by tricking the sorcerer Kei, Ragnar Lodbrok of the Danes who rescues the Princess Thora from an egg-born

Although in India the paths of the hunter and the yogi diverged enormously, elsewhere they remained closely united. Thus the Lord of the Animals is pictured in a typical yogic posture, surrounded by the wild creatures with whom he shares the mystic solidarity of hunter and prey. (Detail of the Gundestrup silver cauldron, Denmark, 4th–3rd century, BC.)

dragon, the Crow brave Scar-Face who is shown the magical weapons of the Morning Star by twin swans, the Sudanese Prince Samba Gana who battles for eight years with the mile-long serpent Issa Beer whose fangs are as elephant tusks, Theseus threading his way toward the Minotaur in the Cretan labyrinth – all these and countless other hero-tales are full of violent action and fabulous, seemingly supernatural events. To what extent they represent prehistoric survival-dramas, or imaginatively embellished versions of such dramas, or, most likely, a combination of the two, is impossible to say, but there can be no doubt that all heroic lore is deeply informed by the memory of what can be called *traumatic sensation*. This comprises all the normal body-sensations and sense-impressions, but in a fearful, brutalized, mutated form. For instance, the common sensation of involuntary breathing becomes traumatic in hyper-ventilation when someone is exposed to mortal risk or the mere suggestion of it. Other physiological effects rapidly follow (dizziness, sweating, tension in the head) and the entire chain-reaction assumes an exaggerated, overwhelming effect which, when we try to describe it, forcefully translates itself into metaphor and imaginative language: 'the headache hit me like a ton of bricks, like I walked into a plate-glass window', etc.

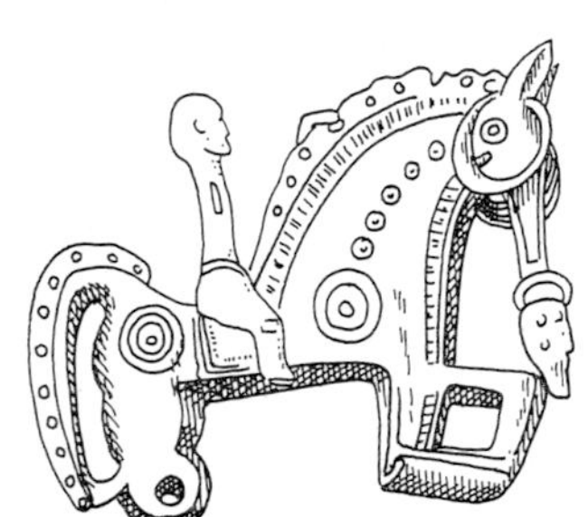

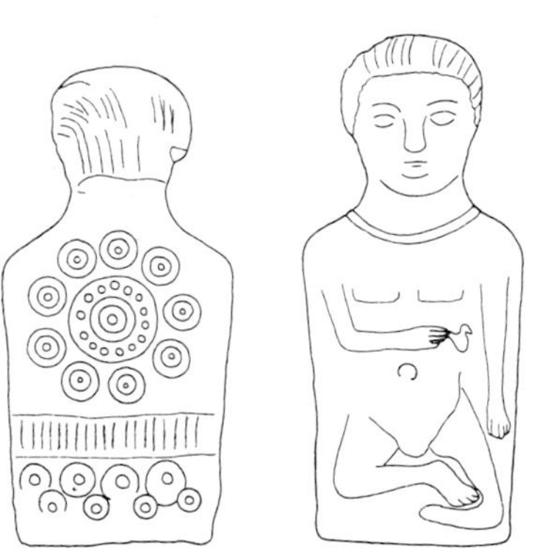

Top: Representing supernatural strength, the horse and the sun are often associated, or even interfused, in heroic lore and legend. (Drawing of Iberian Iron Age brooch.)

Above: As hunter, the hero often entered a trance-state of hypervigilance in which the sensation of his heartbeat was intensified and the body heat concentrated in his upper torso came to be felt like a bird in flight, suspended in the pounding effect of the sun. (Clay statuette from Quilly, in the Loire valley, France.)

At Lascaux, the Magdalenian cave-site that Joseph Campbell called a 'Stone Age cathedral of hunting magic', there is a scene of a man prostrate at the feet of a disembowelled bison, a stunning glimpse of traumatic sensation. Disembowelment, whether of the hunter himself, one of his party or the prey, produced a traumatic effect that imprinted itself on the racial memory in the image of a serpentine mass, the most typical adversary of the first recorded heroes. Every detail of the way hot, heaving bowels look and act translates graphically into the language and imagery of dragon combat (as rereading Beowulf with this in mind will easily prove). Certainly, encounters with actual serpents, beasts of prey, poisonous insects and elemental forces would have added solid empirical content to this psychic effect, but in countless retellings the psychic effect would have predominated, simply due to the free-form tendencies of image and metaphor.

The dragon's breath is hot and foul, like the smell of exposed bowels, yet the dragon guards the solar treasure, the blood-heat. Wounds sting, as does the serpent's bite, even if the serpent is imaginary. Bleeding to death, the body burns and roars, the blood-heat seeming to ebb away in a soft cloudlike suffusion. Initially uncertain of finding in himself anything to match woman's awesome power, man looked to the sun as source of the heat-infused power that sustained him as he stalked the prey, coursing rhythmically in his bloodstream like an interior chant or, under the high stress of fight or flight, pulsating massively in the inferior vena cava, or, as with the fallen man at Lascaux, throbbing in the near-death erection of the penis. The solar-phallic heat was at once the treasure the hero fought to keep and the lethal adversary who threatened it: Maui and Te Tuna interfused.

The array of traumatic sensation could be extended at length: fevers, intense shuddering, hypervigilance, cold-rushes, hyperacuity of the senses, paralysis, blood pounding and roaring in the head, panic attacks, suffocation, near-death experiences, shattered bones, concussions, coma, all forms of wounding, poisoning, burns, near-drowning, all forms of shock, delirium, hallucinations, amnesia. To face and master these effects, the hunter had to match the terror from without with a furious strength from within. Even long after the traumatic impact was no longer a direct and constant threat, heroic stamina was revived and reenacted in hunting rites, initiation ordeals of men's societies, mock battles, war-dances, the grotesque romp of the satyr-play, the fits of the beserkers. Memories of the survival-drama were gradually elaborated into the intricacies of magic and ritual, hero-quest and hero-theme. As Joseph Campbell asserts in the opening pages of *Primitive Mythology*, understanding our own past requires asking 'whether in the human psychosomatic system there have been found any structures or dynamic tendencies to which the origins of myth and ritual might be referred'. Indeed, there have been these aplenty, and the hero, as prehistoric hunter, had to master them all.

Man achieved heroic mastery of himself and nature only to see its value threatened, as if overnight, at the dawn of the Neolithic Revolution, around 8000 BC. Violent and excessive exertion of force, directed by man against nature for thousands of years, now shifted toward his own kind. The discovery of agriculture coincides with the first evidence of intraspecies conflict, man against man. Figures inscribed on the walls of the Valtorta Gorge in Spain show men in vigorous poses armed with bows, no animals. Similar depictions of skirmishes appear at the same time in the Levant and into the Middle East where the ruined fortifications of Jericho attest to massive human conflict. Historians widely agree that the transition from hunter-gatherer to farmer and animal-keeper was (so far) the single most important shift in human evolution. Ironically, the rupture of the hunting bond which had united man to nature and man to man may have been more traumatic in the emotional and spiritual sense than anything man faced in the perils of the hunt.

James Leakey and others maintain that large-scale warfare was impossible among our ancestors before the Neolithic era. With a kind of brutal inevitability agriculture led to stability and possession, which led to commerce, which led to urbanization, which led to war on a large scale. In the hindsight of some 10,000 years, it is unavoidably obvious that violence among our own kind has been escalating ever since. Since 10,000 years is a minute fraction of the hero's experience, we can only imagine how the subconscious force of the preceding millennia works in the male psyche today. With the rupture of the hunting bond, the hero's passion for the kill appears to have turned pathological – and the rest is history.

Pitted against everything from mammoth to mite, man had been unambiguously heroic, but when he turned his violent powers on his own kind, the nature of heroism was forever changed. A skull fractured by a bear's swipe, or a falling rock, is one thing, but fractured by a human foe, it is quite another. The hunter disembowelled by a bison before the eyes of his band was an awesome spectacle with mythic implications and emotional effects far different from those that unfolded when the same injury was inflicted by another man. In shifting from hunter to warrior, the hero found new uses and directions for his male surfeit. His excess of vitality, now liberated from its empathic bond to nature and the animal kingdom, took on an ethical significance in place of its previous survival value. The epochal transformation of man's strength from vital power into moral power is central to the drama of the hero, and still unfolding.

For Mortal to Aid Mortal

The transition from hunter to warrior engaged the entire human species in the dilemma of the *moral dimension* of heroism. No longer is the hero merely a monster-slayer like Cadmus or Beowulf or Saint George, but now he is a man capable of using monstrous excess against his own kind. Hence the warrior becomes, historically, the most influential variant of the hero to appear after our species emerged from the wilds. His later career through chivalry and the romantic path of *amor courtois* into the flowering of humanism defines the modern age, marked by an epic crisis and transformation in our shared concept of humanity itself (see pp. 21–26).

In great measure, the heroic challenge after the Neolithic shift consisted in man's struggle to find an ethical framework for his superfluity of power. Among themselves, warriors developed an unwritten code based on their experiences of facing mutual adversaries. Often meeting death together, dying in each other's arms, covered in blood, they became bound by blood, man to man, as they had previously been bound in mystic communion with the prey. Over time their hunting instincts became converted into a silent knowledge of how men must behave in hand-to-hand combat with their equals on the field of battle. Eventually the heroic code was formulated into the morals and manners of chivalry. The knights of the middle ages were bound to a volunteer system of ethical principles that included, first and foremost, the use of superior strength to protect the weak and helpless. Honour (which means the same as honesty: that is, consistency of word and deed), generosity, fearlessness and self-restraint were all chivalric virtues. In Europe as well as in the great tribal cultures of the American west, these attributes epitomized in the bravest of men had an enormous civilizing influence. Originally challenged to overcome external nature, man continued on the path of the hero as long as he was able to overcome himself and not succumb to the use of his power for selfish ends.

Human skepticism insists that 'human nature' is difficult, if not impossible, to overcome. Perhaps for this reason alone, humanity has viewed the individual who is capable of self-overcoming as more a god than a mortal. As noted above, deification of the hero precludes our compassion for the man of flesh-and-blood. Most heroic tales display a mix of mortal and immortalized elements. Hinun, for instance, is an Iroquois hero clearly invested with Aryan sky-god qualities. He guards the sky with arrows of fire like the thunderbolts of Thor, Indra and Zeus. His wife is Rainbow Woman, herself a superearthly entity. But in the test-tale of his battle with the serpent of the Great Lakes, he is accompanied by a young brave, Gunnodoyak, who is swallowed whole by the serpent. Here Gunnodoyak, like Maui interfused with Te Tuna, represents the true human hero whose trials are marked by traumatic sensation and the mastery of his own internal, metabolic functions, including kundalini, the serpent power. Intimate with blood and bowels, the young brave represents the somatic values divested from the transcendental, immortalized figure of Hinun.

Ascribing a divine paternity to the hero has perennially been a tactic in patriarchal recensions of oral, somatically-based lore. Because establishing the father was so often difficult, insemination was ascribed to a superhuman male progenitor. Among the classical Greek heroes, those cited as having Zeus as father were Perseus (with Danae), Herakles (with Alcmene; although she also has a twin of mortal parentage, Iphikles), Pollux (with Leda, although Castor is again the mortal twin of the union), King Minos (with Europa), Amphion, who raised the walls of Thebes with music (with Antiope), Lacedaemon, chief of Sparta (with a 'star-maiden') and Dardanus, founder of the Trojans (also with a 'star-maiden'). Aeneas, another famous hero of the Trojan lineage, was the offspring of a mixed mating between the goddess Aphrodite and Anchises, a mortal and mere shepherd. Outside the Greek lore, clear accounts of mixed parentage are extremely rare: one exception being Manawyddan, a Celtic hero, born of the union of Llyr, a river god, and Penardum, a mortal woman. In Hindu lore, the young archer Arjuna, warrior-hero of the *Mahabharata,* is the son of the sky-god Indra and a nymph, Kunti.

Regardless of his parentage, the hero must always exhibit one specific trait to be deemed truly a hero. His capacity for benign aggression must be directed toward aiding and assisting others, as much as protecting them from obvious dangers. This aspect of heroic morality was beautifully stated by Cicero, a pagan voice who inspired Petrarch in reshaping heroic values into the secular philosophy of humanism. In his Tusculan Disputations, Cicero wrote: *Deus est mortali juvare mortalem.* 'For mortal to aid mortal, this is god.' The many angles and opportunities for this aid constitute a whole other dimension of heroic activity.

Much of history consists of the fact that we do not know the facts, especially when it comes to the origins of many activities, some as simple as striking fire with flint, others as complex as astronomy. Throughout the world, wherever skills and improvements have been introduced to humanity, heroes have been identified as the benefactors. Often vested with the attributes of gods bringing transhuman wisdom, they serve totally human needs in a totally human manner. Technically, these are the 'culture-heroes', a huge company of innovators, experimentors, benefactors and educators who fall into two main categories, ameliorative and ethnogenic.

During the Neolithic Revolution, humankind developed a whole array of new skills such as pottery-making, blacksmithing, irrigation and trapping and taming of animals. These are feats of adaptation which is, as noted above, the forte of the female, although more often credited to *homo faber,* 'man the maker'. Aggression against nature and the wild kingdoms assumed a lower priority as a survival-skill when the male was demoted from hunter to gamekeeper. Tales of monster-slayers, recalling the millennial struggle of man to protect his kind, continue to be told, but in the context of increasingly socialized culture, their character changes. In one direction, they are adapted to confer prestige on those regents, theocrats and patriarchal headsmen who now emerge, taking care of business now that there is business to conduct as a side-effect of agriculture. The ameliorative culture-hero is the one who improves on things, takes over and manages situations. This leads rapidly to the 'law-giver', be it as Manu among the Aryan Hindus or Manco Capac among the Peruvians. He is the hero turned champion, manu, cosmocrater and authority-figure – not genuinely a hero any more, yet invested with the animal traits of his primitive forebears. Markings, ornamentation, masks and animal skins that served him for camouflage and imitation in the bush become royal regalia, seen today in the ermine stole of Queen Elizabeth. The borrowing continues as well in the strange menagerie found on heraldic crests.

In another direction, the hunter subdued to the pastoral life metamorphosed into another kind of hero, the dying and resurrecting god. Divested of animal powers, he becomes identified with the vegetal kingdom. In this transitional mythology figures like Tammuz, Attis and Adonis, spectral and unconvincing in their ambiguous status between god, plant and human, become prominent in the Fertile Crescent where agriculture developed to its highest sophistication. These gods are morbid, even pathetic, completely subjugated to the rhythmic, seasonal spell of the Goddess. They are emasculated sons of the Great Mother who die and are reborn out of her fertile loins. It is very rare to find accounts of the hero as a vegetative deity with any heroic character-traits intact. Nevertheless, this transitional version of the quasi-deific hero persists and eventually gathers its own strength and character. Later he assumes odd characters in the mould of the 'wild man' from the backwoods, sometimes retaining archaic Dionysiac features: John Barleycorn, Robin Goodfellow, and Herne the Hunter, a deranged, antlered, horn-blowing horseman who haunts Windsor Forest in England, himself an isolated straggler who properly belongs to the spectral horde of the Wild Hunt.

In non-European cultures, the benefits of pastoral life are closely related to the earlier, monster-slaying feats of the hero. In a continuation of the Polynesian account of Maui's battle with the monster eel, Te Tuna, Maui is instructed by his mother, Hau-Hega, to bury the monster's head beside a post in the corner of the family hut. Later, a sprout appears, the first precious shoot of the coconut tree. Maui, acting as *homo faber*, splits the nut to fashion bowls for drinking the milk, and initiates a boastful song in praise of this magical conversion of monstrous foe into life-sustaining nourishment.

Among the Greeks, agriculture was said to have been introduced by the Goddess Demeter, whose cult was celebrated at Eleusis. The sacred rites observed there were foundational to Attic culture by close association with civic customs in which the Goddess transferred her chthonic, life-nurturing powers to the male lineage of Athenian kings. Gaia herself gives birth out of the earth to Erechthonios, first in the lineage of clan-kings who raised the Parthenon. Here is a rare, perhaps unique instance of a 'politically correct' transition to patriarchy. Cecrops, the Athenian king who 'fathers' Erechthonios, is pictured as a man with a snake's tail, archaic evidence that he is a hero who has mastered and merged with the dragon-powers. It is said that he arbitrates in the conflict between Athena, matriarchy, seen through a masculine lens, and Poseidon, high god of patriarchy and deific prototype of the warrior, thundermaker and horseman. Cecrops dissolved the matrilineal rule whereby sons are called by their mother's family name, and he enforced the strict joining one man to one woman, insuring the identification of male progeny. Commentators of the time assert that before these civic changes it was not possible for men to know their fathers.

Among the Murray Islanders of Australasia, Badu and Moa are twin culture-heroes who introduce gardening and the use of fish-weirs. In neighbouring New Guinea, Naga is an ancestral chief who instructs the men in the making of masks

The Chinese Emperor Shennong exemplifies the shaggy, archaic culture-hero who emerges from nature, a wild man attributed with teaching traditional practices of finding food or concocting medicines. (Illustrated from *San-ts'ai t'u-hui*, 1607.)

and teaches the songs and dances to be performed in the *kwod*, the ceremonial ground within the communal habitat which carries the mana, or sacred power, of the boundless hunting territory outside. Kwioam of the same region is a culture-hero who lives in a matrilineal society with his mother, by whose counsel he organizes the male warrior-societies (phratries) into sacred lineages. Likewise, the native American culture-hero, Hiawatha, a brave of Iroquois stock who probably lived during the 14th century, is credited with forming the Grand League of Five Nations, of which there is some historical evidence.

Far more distant in time stand figures like the Egyptian culture-hero, Imhotep, a quasi-historical figure dated around 2900 BC in the reign of Zoser. He appears to have been a jack of all trades: architect, scribe, physician, master of occult arts such as geometry and astrology. One of his contemporaries in China would have been Shennong, an early ruler associated with the time of the Yellow Emperor, circa 3000 BC. He introduced certain foods and the manner of cooking them and prepared medicines from healing herbs which he was able to detect because he had a transparent stomach that allowed him to observe every detail of his digestion. Tales of Taoist adepts able to see into their own bodies were common in that epoch. Nevertheless, Shennong died rather gruesomely after ingesting the wrong kind of grass – an event which no doubt happened thousands of times in the trial-and-error experimentations required to discover edible food in the wilds.

The advances or improvements provided by the culture-hero can apply both to small domestic and ritual matters as well as large-scale civilizing activities. Olofat, a clan hero of the Caroline Islands, the son of a sky-father and a mortal woman, taught the intricacies of tattooing and hairdressing, as well as tilling the soil. Often cosmogenic and heroic elements are mixed in the fame figure: Wisaka, widely celebrated in North America, is a deity who created the people and then taught them hunting, sports, song and dance. He also belongs to one of the special class civilizing heroes who promises to return to his people at a later time, should they forget the ways of survival and celebration he has taught them.

Often the culture-hero stands apart from a competing authority-figure, the champion, who appears in the same account, as seen with Gilgamesh and Enkidu; then again, the hero himself sometimes degenerates into a tyrant. In China the folk-hero Fan Wen, Fan the Hammer, is a shamanic lord known throughout the land for forging a magical sword on two carp who had transformed themselves into whetstones. On one occasion, he put himself in the service of the Emperor, Fan I, solely to assist in improving the life of the people. Fan Wen instructed the imperial work-force in how to build ramparts and ditches, and then, prompted by the Emperor, he introduced new weapons and clever battle strategies. Eventually promoted to commander of the imperial armies, Fen Wen jeopardized his own position in the patriarchal system by challenging the loyalty of the Crown Prince. Ultimately tempted by the taste of power, he poisoned the Crown Prince and set himself up as a cruel tyrant. Chinese and Japanese lore often present examples of the hero corrupted by his own power, contrasting to the heroes of Greek tragedy, like Oedipus, whose downfall is either due to the missapplication of power (Oedipus mistakenly kills his own father) or to the overwhelming burden of suffering that comes as the price for having it at all (Oedipus blinds himself physically to the effects of his moral failings).

Many of the ameliorative culture-heroes are obviously drawn from shamanic traditions. In the Amazon, Uaica is a master hunter, closely identified with the jaguar, who discovers a bark-potion useful in feats of high sorcery, a close parallel to Yakut and Siberian heroes who ingest fly agaric to achieve the superfluity of forces required for transport to other dimensions where they find lost articles or rescue the accursed or ailing. Metallurgy is closely linked with the shamanic arts, and the smith as a hero appears in figures as diverse as the Finnish Ilmarinen, a hero of the *Kalevala*, and the African Gu, first man of the Fon of Dahomey. Among the Hebrews, Bezaleel was the smith charged by Moses with the task of constructing the Ark of the Covenant, a clear-cut example of a patriarchal champion commanding the services of a native artificer.

The second class of culture-heros is the 'ethnogenic' type, attributed with the founding of races. Herakles himself falls into this category. Like many a hero, he is said to have travelled far and wide, occasionally entering into a marriage with dynastic implications. Legend has it that he travelled to the Urals where one night as he slept his mares strayed away in the dark. Searching for them he came upon a 'viper-maiden' who eventually bore him three sons. One of these was Scythes, the progenitor of the Scythians, from whom descended a line of warrior kings. The Scythian love of gold-working recalls the motif of Herakles as a solar hero.

Throughout the middle ages, both the French and German people identified their heroic ancestor as Hector, the slain hero of the Iliad; as did other races as diverse as the Bretons, Flemings, Scandinavians, Italians, Normans, Spaniards. This is remarkable, since legend clearly reports that Hector was slain by Achilles and his only offspring killed. This proves that the Europeans were not honouring themselves with genetic descent from the heroes of antiquity: rather, they found prestige in the heroic supervitality invested with noble traits, so potent and enduring that it overflowed through the centuries with the effect of a generative bond.

Tragedy and Transfiguration

Both in his own eyes and in the eyes of the world, the hero is defined by how he behaves and what he believes. The second factor is truly decisive, for what he believes about himself and about the effect of his actions, both immediate and ultimate, determines if he is truly a hero *in character* and not merely in the outward display of his acts. As we have seen, in archaic and legendary accounts, the moral dimension of the hero is not an issue. Enkidu knows no right or wrong, merely the awful confusion of becoming a human, a socialized animal. Beowulf is a great hero, indeed, regardless of his acts and attitudes outside the fen, which anyway do not interest us. We do not question the serene benevolence of Yu, master of floods, the Chinese culture-hero who founded the Hsia Dynasty. He is known for his feat of controlling the rivers to preserve the people and for his selfless devotion to civic duties, and that's it. Even though we see in Samson an all-too-human temper, we recognize that his tantrum, bringing down the temple, is just another instance of heroic excess, like the wrath of Achilles and the battle-fever of Cuchullain; and there is not much more to it than that.

As history advances, all this changes and the hero assumes ethical depths and existential features that reflect our human predicament in general and the plight of the male in particular. These character-changes first occur in Greek tragedy where the former heroes of the Homeric Era – Oedipus, Agamemnon, Ajax, Orestes, Herakles and others – now find themselves on the stage of the social theatre, facing family feuds, sorting out passion and betrayal, enduring crises of conscience. There is domestic violence and plenty of it. Exposed in the arena of collective karma, the hero does odd things, overreacts and miscalculates. Exhibiting nobility and generosity in excess of the average person, he also displays a fatal fallibility, *hamartia*. He rages and tackles insoluble moral problems. Mostly, he suffers, right out in the open. For the tragic persona he has become, heroic feats and monster-tests no longer matter, for his own suffering has become the supreme monstrosity with which he must contend. In Greek tragedy, the heroic quest becomes internalized as a moral drama and the man of antiquity becomes psychological, like us, today. Kerenyi observed that the cult and myth of the hero contain tragedy in germ.

Hybris, it is said, is the main cause of the hero's troubles: a word usually taken to mean 'arrogance, excessive pride'. But in no way is the hero proud, at least not in the Christian sense of pride as a sin that 'goeth before a fall'. We recall that the hero is marked by the *excess of vital force* he raises and manages – or not. *Hybris* really derives from the Greek verb *hybrizein*, found in Homer, where it means to run riot and reckless like a force of nature, as when rivers overflow their banks in a raging storm. In the *Odyssey*, describing Penelope's suitors, Homer uses it for wanton violence and the insolence that so often goes with it. *Hybrisma* is outrage, violation, rape, serious bodily harm or a loss at sea. Thus, the primary mark of the hero in Greek drama is not a moral defect of pride, but a vital-emotional excess, exactly of the kind he manifests elsewhere as *furor, wut, ferg*, the frenzy and surfeit unique to man. In tragedy, *hybris* is the counterweight to the enormity of the hero's suffering which comes upon him because he is engaged in human dilemmas with no clear and final solutions.

In Sophocles' *Ajax*, the protagonist runs riot, beheading a flock of sheep, and the chorus warns Menelaus of losing his temper and committing similar outrages. Agamemnon, in his turn, warns he'll wreak havoc on anyone who gets reckless: i.e., he threatens excess with more of the same. Caught in their hybris, all the heroes are 'overreacting'. Struggling with emotions he cannot manage, Ajax exhibits typical heroic scorn and impiety, claiming that any coward can be victorious if the gods get behind him. When Athene comes to assist him in battle, he dismisses her! By contrast, Odysseus is a model of sobriety and caution, though selfish and ungenerous compared to Ajax. Sophocles shows Ajax's suicide on stage, involving the audience directly in man's violence turned against himself. Ajax was a national hero in Attica, to whom many families traced their descent, so the spectacle must have hit home, ruthlessly. His final speech is without bravado, heroic and humble.

In Greek tragedy, the spectacle of the tragic hero gives strength, cathartic release and inspiration. It infuses life-force and inspires the will to learn, courageously, from what life forces upon us. The hero learns from his suffering or he does not learn enough, or soon enough, but the community does. He faces despair, injustice, with no way of excusing it, arguing himself out or appealing to a higher power. The hero forges humanity in his own conscience, for he is the one in whom vitality becomes transformed into that innermost core of moral integrity at whose centre one finds what Joseph Campbell called the 'hero-heart'.

In the early Middle Ages, the hero both in his role as warrior and as poet or bard was often endowed with occult powers. Here he appears to escape from the clutches of a monster by performing a feat of magical flight, following the instructions in a grimoire or manual of practical magic. (Early 11th century manuscript.)

Tragedy humanized the hero and opened the path that would eventually lead him beyond his role as warrior. As the way he died and suffered changed, the hero discovered something entirely new. Since time before reckoning, he had fought and died hand to hand and eye to eye with the prey, the monster or human foe, who was always a close match. This continued throughout the Age of Chivalry, the era in European history most richly embroidered with heroic lore, but as if by extraordinary foresight the heroes of that much-celebrated time were already preparing for what would come when the chivalric ideal was outmoded and outgrown. Specific technological events would eventually compel the shift, incurring a sea-change and transfiguration for the hero.

One such event was the discovery of gunpowder, initially made around 1000 AD by the Chinese who used it for firework displays, then independently reinvented by a German monk in 1314. Then, in 1430 the first cast-iron gun was introduced. From the middle of the 15th century massive technological efforts on all fronts of life show *homo faber* in a frenzy of invention, producing everything from the battleship (1598) to the barometer (1643). As man began to mechanize his world, the career of the hero shifted direction toward invention and exploration. He assumed more and more the role of the explorer, inventor, scientist, physician, engineer; but to a large extent these new roles were a huge distraction from the moral development of the hero, which had already taken its own independent course. Some time between the 7th and the 12th centuries, however, man had already entered upon a new path. Even before technology and political change deprived him of his customary habits of fighting and dying, he had been exploring an ingenious alternative: a whole new realm of conflict, a whole other way to die.

In Dante's *Inferno*, one of the doomed lovers, Francesca da Rimini, is made to say: *Amor condusse noi ad una morte*, 'Love led us to one death'. It was woman, of all

Evolving into the lover, the hero became the most well-known figure (actually, a celebrity) in the popular culture of East and West alike. Here Bahran Gur woos an Indian princess in the Black Pavilion, a setting reminiscent of the Arthurian 'castle marvellous'. (Miniature from Nizami's *Khamsa*, 1445.)

creatures, who opened the way the hero would take from classical warrior to modern male. *Antar*, an Arabian romance based on materials from the 7th century, depicts a chevalier who exalts his beloved, Alba, as guide and protectress of his martial adventures. From *Her* he draws a surfeit of supernatural power and, in turn, dedicates to her all his heroic acts and contests with overwhelming foes, monstrous and human alike. The hero of Antar represented for that time a moral code independent of the religious virtues and obligations proposed by Christian and Islamic doctrines. He presented a model which rapidly developed in the West, especially in Southern France: the knight dedicated to the tests of and triumphs over carnal love, profane passion.

Historians often state in a ho-hum manner that romantic love was a literary invention, as if everyone knows that love sufficient to transform the world, and transfigure humanity in both the sexes, could come off the printed page. Paolo and Francesca, the illicit lovers in Dante, are first discovered not *in flagrante delicto* (as the box office would have it), but reading a book together. A great part of the hero's role in inventing romantic love was that he learned how to read and sing, he became literate. A long tradition supported this development. Chrétien de Troyes, author of several chivalric romances, declared that Greece was the origin of three great adventures: romance, knighthood and 'clergie', by which he meant learning. Classical tradition itself showed heroes like Achilles and Herakles being tutored in the fine arts of writing and rhetoric, and Homer asserted that a clear and forceful speaker of words was equivalent to a doer of courageous deeds. Through the middle ages, the *prudentia* expected of the hero as complement to his *fortitudo* became more and more refined into *sapientia*, wisdom. Training in warrior skills was to be complemented by training of the sensibility through written culture: *armas y letras* in the Spanish code. The result was a flowering of lyric and romance (a long

In a much-celebrated allegory, the sleeping hero is confronted by the figures of two women, representing the paths of literature (book) and aesthetics (flowers) toward which the warrior turned at the dawn of humanism. (Raphael: so-called *Dream of Scipio*, c. 1505.)

tale in vernacular prose) on a truly magnificent scale, the literary renaissance of the 12th century.

At the centre of this vast cultural breakthrough were two figures, a man and a woman, hero and lady. The idealization of woman by her knight has rightfully been considered as one of the most astounding moral, cultural, sociological, psychological and spiritual shifts in human history. For the hero, *amor courtois*, courtly love, was a school of manners in which his self-image became entirely transfigured. Just as the passage from hunter to warrior had entailed the evolution of a whole set of values, now another passage began and nothing less than a new morality emerged. The heroic path now became the path of the heart, of passion and intimacy. Chivalric tales of knights fighting dragons or jousting against formidable adversaries remained popular fare, but the subtext contained the true story. Usually, the dramatic tension of the narrative hinged on the conflict of loyalties facing the hero: he must weigh his feudal allegiance to his lord against his dedication to his lady, who was often enough the lawful wife of the lord. Now the well-known love-triangle appears, for instance in Arthur-Lancelot-Guinevere, a complete transfiguration of the archaic triangle of hero-woman-monster. Often the hero is tested by the choice between desire for his lady and longing for the time-tried challenges of his masculine power, or by the choice of humility over manly pride. To save his lady's honour, Lancelot had to accept the indignity of riding in a cart, something a knight worthy of the name would never do. A moment's hesitation in deciding convinced Guinevere that his love was less than perfect. The overwhelming force here is human passion, romantic love, invested by Gottfried of Strassburg with all the markings of religious torment. For Tristan and Isolde their love is the bread and wine of an intimate communion, overtly displacing the communion and atonement offered by the Church. The hero attains the highest expression of his masculine power by surrendering it, for Woman is no longer the helpless victim he rescues from the dragon: she herself is his deliverance.

In the troubadour idiom, She is called *Domna*: lord and superior, she who dominates the man in the sense that she alone determines the purity of his motive and the value of his actions. Socially, Domna is a rival to the feudal lord to whom the knight typically owes his loyalty and his life. Spiritually, she is erected as a higher power in a feat of psychological transformation that profoundly affected Western culture. In a consummate act of self-surrender, the hero renders himself powerless and stays that way, unless his power is reflected back to him through Her. Previously he had found in death the perfect measure and seal of his heroic will, now it is love itself that leads him to another kind of death. In Gottfried, the *liebestod*, love-death, is the culminating moment of Tristan's quest. No more a warrior seeking his equal for a final match of strength, the hero dies in the arms of his beloved, and she in his, transported to that dimension of final intimacy to which death itself is merely an accessory.

As the hero evolved into the lover, a new language evolved from his experience. The chevalier and his lady conversed in a subtle, sophisticated code preserved in troubadour lyric – an arcane vocabulary that did not, for the most part, find its way into modern French. *Amor courtois* was called in the Occitanian idiom of Provence, *fin amors*: not fine or perfect love but 'sincere, not obliged', not required by social rules or any demands external to the power exchanged by the lovers. Even strong physical passion, viewed as a mere symptom of the procreative urge, was considered as external. Troubadour language made excruciating distinctions regarding true passion and the right manner to express it. *Chauzimen* was the discretion that prevented the lovers from wasting themselves by the excess to which their passions might naturally tempt them. It was the heroic virtue of self-restraint, essential to the management of male excess, now applied to the overpowering attraction between the hero and his lady. *Mezura* was constantly invoked as essential to all romantic discourse and intercourse: temperance, balance, with a nuance of elegance. In submitting to love, the hero exchanged prowess for sensibility, *enans*: literally, superior manners. He rejected *drut*, carnal love for its own sake, and *folor*, virility in its base form, seeking instead to find in his very passions a path toward *proenza*, insight or recognition in the sense of a soul-felt rapport with his lady, and *pretz*, loving esteem, worthiness, the dignity conferred by intimate contact with woman and her mysteries. In place of Christian *charitas*, he sought *cortezia*, self-esteem reflected in beautiful manners. Moderated in self-love by the reflection of his Beloved, the hero now managed his masculine charisma as he had formerly managed his rage. In doing so, however, he did not renounce force completely, but he only continued to undertake adventures and tests in the service of his Domna. From her he received supernatural protection and the permission to use violent force. Many of the troubadours who developed this exquisite code of manners and the language to express it were also seasoned fighters, adept with sword and lance.

Fin amors involved an entire system of interpersonal values independent of Christian ethics. The hero in love valued *fizanze*, confidence, not fidelity. The ennobling love he sought, *amors enansa*, was finally a spiritual gift, superior to anything that noble blood or Christian grace could offer. The mark of achieving it was *virtu*, authenticity, pure and simple. In the Renaissance *virtu* became the moral signature of the courtier, the enlightened, humanized man of the world who was none other than the hero himself, man reborn in a new image. Along the way to this transfiguration, the hero had achieved through the medium of the Domna an array of experiences which can be imagined as modifications of the primary heroic asset, vitality, excess of the life-force. In this way, the demonstration of male surfeit outlived its aggressive phase. It was no longer fulfilled in acts of power but in the power of acts inspired by deep personal love, esthetic sensibility and humanistic vision.

Perhaps the ultimate gain, the highest social and spiritual achievement of the chivalry, was simply the inception of *amistat*, friendship between the sexes. René Nelli, a poet and scholar of Occitanian culture, has proposed that the male devotees of *fin amors* found with woman a bond of friendship previously and exclusively known between men themselves. Since Paleolithic times, men had revered the Goddess for her life-nurturing largesse, yet feared her in her mortal form as the one who lured him to where she bled from her secret recesses and the mother who often bore him into birth covered in that same taboo-charged blood. To compete with this mystery, men in archaic cults had resorted to practices of ritual bloodletting, circumcision and subincision, investing themselves with the taboo nature confers on all women and, paradoxically, becoming true men by imitating how women bleed. In death and wounding, the warrior-hero forged a blood-bond with his kin and even with the foe who 'blessed' him – *blesser* in French means to 'wound'. Orders of knighthood were commonly bound by blood-ties but even these were not strong enough to prevent man from ultimately making that heroic transition beyond blood to its transcendent components, ephemeral passion and enduring love.

Outside of Europe, this transition did not occur in anywhere near as dramatic a fashion. In many parts of the world, the hero remained arrested in his Stone Age status right down to the beginning of the 20th Century: in America, for instance, where the pure type of the 'noble savage', every inch a hero and warrior by the Homeric standard, persisted until he and his kind were driven to near extinction by the genocidal aggression of the colonials and frontiersmen. In Central America, the era of chivalry and *amor courtois* corresponded temporally to the rise of the Aztecs, a warrior culture in which heroism on the battlefield was carried to psychotic excess. Nonetheless, among the Aztecs there existed forms of lyrical love-poetry as tender and compelling as anything one can find in the troubadour cult. Historically and culturally, there seems to be an odd parallel between high violence and high esthetics, both of which are indications that male surfeit has been developed to an extreme and decadent degree. Masculine beauty, a classical mark of the hero, seems to thrive in those cultures where masculine power is valorized almost to a pathological extent. The heroic culture of the Celts also displayed this dual glorification of power and beauty. Cuchullain is described in numerous accounts as so radiantly beautiful that the sight of him is practically unbearable.

In Japan, also, the cult and mystique of the samurai closely paralleled the epoch of chivalry in the West, but instead of Romantic Love it was the Buddhist concept of the Void that dominated the morality and esthetics of the feudal courts. Around 700, the national chronicles began to be compiled out of massive oral lore derived from the traditions of the *katari-be*, bards who sang the exploits of clan heroes and mounted aristocratic warriors. Prince Yamato, one hero of the era, is the exact counterpart to King Arthur.

The Heian period (794–1185) saw the emergence of the samurai as a folk-hero possessing a unique mix of masculine charisma and feminine sensibility. The heroic acceptance of death was ritually observed in *sepukku*, suicide performed as the honourable alternative to disgrace or dishonour. Often the samurai recited a spontaneous *haiku*, a three-lined Zen poem, as a final elegant act of self-composure before disembowelling himself. To live and die beautifully was the primary criterion of conduct for the aristocratic hero whose spirit was permeated with *aware*, the sense of the sad, exquisite transience of all things. Buddhist compassion for all sentient beings here took the extreme and decadent form of an esthetic of polished impersonality. Passional romantic engagement of the kind that transfigured the hero in the West was impossible in Japan, because life in its dream-like transitoriness did not really afford the opportunity to fathom the depths of the Other. One and other were the same in the Void, a dimension where the unitary love-death was impossible because there was, ultimately, no one there – certainly no one particular and personal – to undergo either love or death.

The Ever-changing Quest

Rather like a chameleon, the hero changes with his surroundings, his time and his sociocultural environment. As a medium and moving index of our common experience, he is susceptible to being overwhelmed by the very conditions he reflects, especially when these conditions become hugely or grotesquely magnified so that the moral orientation of the hero to his situation is difficult, if not impossible, to discern. In the war in Vietnam, for instance, the elusiveness of the Viet Cong made it impossible for a soldier entering a jungle village to know if he was out to slaughter innocent peasants or eliminate a treacherous foe. Returning home tormented and broken, many Vietnam vets had to face shame and rejection while continuing to struggle inwardly with the impossibility of knowing whether or not they had acted, or could have acted, heroically in certain situations.

Man, the male of the species, is shaped by the hero mythos, and the mythos in turn acts as a powerful directive in society at large. For most of the hero's career, his story was told orally. Heroic narrative in written form begins with Gilgamesh and runs through Homer and the *Mahabharata* to the medieval romances with unbroken continuity until the invention of printing; then jumps into another scale. As early as the 10th century, heroic narrative began to change radically *as the texts became more and more contemporary with the events they described.* It is one thing for a Merovingian king, reaching back over 1800 years, to claim Hector as his ancestor, and another for the latest hero on the evening news to be adopted as a role-model by, say, all the teenage males in the land. Even semi-legendary figures scripted into national heroes, such as El Cid, have a way of persisting in the imagination that cannot be compared to the fame of historical figures whose last names are emblazoned above the tumultuous crowds they incite: Zapata, Mao, Che, Castro, Mandela. Hector is more a hero than Castro, not because he is so far removed in time that he becomes adaptable to whatever one may wish to imagine of him – certainly not, for the character and actions of Hector are stable through the ages, while the character and actions of Castro are relative, dubious, constantly shifting in value. Hector and Lancelot and El Cid are figures who survive in the human imagination in a way historical heroes cannot. It remains to be seen if Castro strikes anyone as a hero in the year 3800 AD.

In short, the hero is vulnerable to the way his tale is told and interpreted. In the so-called modern age, marked by the dominance of technological and ideological developments on a global scale, he is at risk of being overwhelmed by the very means used to represent him, to perpetuate his fame. He, the master of excess and the embodiment of superfluity, stands at risk of being hyped to death. Consequently, man, the male, has to face a crisis of identity and respond, somehow, to the compelling need to redefine his quest.

The crisis was prepared by man's moral advance during the Renaissance. The flowering of the hero as lover, courtier and humanist brought our species to a kind of threshold. As explosive weaponry for use in large-scale conflicts began to be introduced, the hero filled with humanistic vision had to look beyond the old expressions of power to new challenges, new frontiers. Invention and exploration became the two main professional careers for a man to pursue if he wanted to

In the 19th century, the hero's excess led him to look beyond the confines of the earth. In the 20th, what he had only imagined became a reality. (Illustration from Jules Verne, *From the Earth to the Moon*, 1893.)

achieve something heroic, while the career of the military man took a detour that led away from a genuine, morally inspired heroism toward the machinations and power-politics of global overkill. This course of action was epitomized in a stunning image in Stanley Kubrick's film, *Dr Strangelove*: the cowboy bombardier whipping his chaps as he rides the atomic bomb out of the belly of the B-52 and down to the Russian target. No man can be a hero with that kind of *hybris* between his legs.

Technological innovations, both in theory and practice, demonstrate the heroic faculties of Odysseus, the wily, the man of wit and ingenuity. The Industrial Revolution highlighted men of science and engineers as the great heroes of civilization: Newton, Watt, Edison, Ford. The idea of mastering nature in the cause of Progress belongs, however, to an abstract and patriarchal ideology totally alien to the code of the hero. Once again, it is necessary to distinguish the accomplishments of the champion from the efforts of the hero. The latter will usually be found making advances and breakthroughs in some discreditable or unorthodox manner, challenging taboos or risking everything to master a dire and desperate situation. Figures in medical history like Semmelweiss, who brought gynecology out of the dark ages, remain true to heroic ethics. In medicine, man gets to apply his aggressive abilities to fight monstrous and often lethal forces which threaten the survival of the species. In classical lore, the centaur Chiron was tutor to Herakles and the hero is often associated with healing.

Explorations to the extremes – the north and south poles, the depths of the sea, the top of Everest – were natural attractions for man seeking ways to test his surfeit and outdo himself. The story of Sir Richard Burton's quest for the source of the Nile is a stunning hero tale, rendered on film as *The Mountains of the Moon*. Burton's contest with Speke over who discovered what is yet another instance of the struggle between champion (Speke) and hero (Burton), demonstrating clearly how the hero's fulfilment, if he has any, is always private and subjective, rather than validated by the authorities of the day.

Another new role that emerged for the hero in recent times is the revolutionary whose personal power and vision determine the fate of his people. At best, he appears in the figure of men like Gandhi and Mandela who promote social revolution by nonviolent means and democratic vision. At worst, he becomes an ideological cipher charged with the desperate and dangerous aspirations of the mass-man, the faceless crowd. Stalin, one of the greatest genocidal maniacs of all time, is still a hero to millions in the former Soviet Union. In his brilliant study, *The Mass Psychology of Fascism*, Wilhelm Reich exposed the pathology of powerlessness which allows men of little strength and no character to be elevated to positions of supreme power by the masses who cannot claim any power for themselves. This is the most dangerous detour of heroism, the transmogrification in which a man falsely empowered by others can at one and the same time be absolved from his own violence and unconditionally delegated to use it against others. Here the heroic code of honour and autonomy are utterly forgotten, and in their place there arises that pathological deviation, the hero-cult. In a series of lectures delivered in 1840, Thomas Carlyle promoted 'hero-worship' with fundamentalist fervour, citing Odin, Mohammed, Shakespeare, Luther, John Knox, Samuel Johnson and Cromwell as exemplars. His fanatical and uncritical endorsement of the 'transcendental admiration of great men' was a terrible nadir for the hero and effectively prepared the atmosphere for the Nazi-Aryan cult of male supremacy.

At the beginning of the 20th century, the heroic quest turned to the mysteries of the human mind. Freud identified man with the Greek hero, Oedipus, who was daring enough to solve the riddle of the sphinx but then blinded himself in denial of the human consequences of his self-knowledge. (Ingres: *Oedipus and the Sphinx*, c. 1826.)

The hero shows us how the male claims his power, his virility, and where he goes with it. He can create hell on earth, or he can use it to penetrate hell and return with its secrets and riches. The theme of the *Nekyia*, the journey to the underworld, occurs in Gilgamesh, Homer and Scandinavian myth where the warrior-hero, Woden, descends into hell to undergo an initiatory ordeal and receive the sacred formulas of the runes. Mass-psychologies that elevate psychotic maniacs to world power are rooted in this same hell-realm, the racial unconscious, and efforts to penetrate it represent a continuation of the *Nekyia* in our time. Freud prefaced *The Interpretation of Dreams* with a line from Virgil: 'If I cannot persuade the higher powers, then I will shift the infernal regions.' The heroicization of Freud as the lonely pioneer who allegedly opened the gates to the unconscious is itself so extensive a myth that it may be more remarkable than anything the man actually accomplished. In any case, the saga of Freud as courageous hero fitted well with his pretensions. On the one hand, Freud equated himself with Oedipus, and on the other, he confided privately that he felt closest in spirit to a great *conquistador* like Pizarro. Clearly, Freud was no hero but an intellectual champion defending the values of male-dominance. His ally and later adversary, C. G. Jung, was more of a hero in his obvious emotional dependence on woman as muse and guide. While Freud proposed the fixation of infantile libido on the mother, Jung affirmed the more noble and interactive scenario in which woman serves the formation of the male psyche by representing the anima, a concept suggested to him by his first mistress, Sabina Spielrein. Other figures in depth psychology who could perhaps qualify even more strongly as true hero-types are Wilhelm Reich, who claimed to have discovered the orgone, a form of cosmic supervitality, and Sandor Ferenzci, who encouraged sexual enlightenment and genuine affective bonding between patient and analyst. Reich's late experiments with weather-control link him to the contest with elemental forces, typical of archaic heroes. Both he and Ferenzci were radicals and outsiders, as heroes often are.

Unfortunately, few heroes in the contemporary scene are willing to go as deep into themselves as may be required for the hero-image to be resurrected – yet again – into a new, daring and future-oriented model of moral excellence. In contemporary culture and the media, athletes, cops and hard action matinee idols remain the most consistent heroes, simply because they get the most hype. Of these, the athlete alone has a long-standing claim to legitimacy. In ancient Greece, the Olympic games were instituted in the same era as tragedy, and equally invested with civic value. Athletes exhibit mastery of excessive and exceptional forces, rare bodily discipline and physical beauty, and they maintain in many cases the heroic code of manners which honours the adversary as an equal. Cops, on the other hand, are easily co-opted into champions of male authority, so heroic status for them depends much more upon the situation in which they are portrayed. A cop who simply busts the bad guys because they are doing wrong is less a hero than the one who risks everything to fight corruption in his own ranks: hence the enduring popularity of police dramas involving split loyalties, or films such as *Serpico* and *Prince of the City* which show the agonistic and often tragic struggle of a lone individual to uphold honour and integrity when the lines between right and wrong are not clearly drawn.

Through the ages the heroic quest has varied in many ways while the heroic code of morality has remained profoundly consistent. Feats of strength have been superseded by strength of character, so that today we expect to find an ethical or humane dimension in the personality of the hero, no matter how impressive his actions or achievements might be. Lacking this, he is not truly a hero in the contemporary sense. Figures like Henry David Thoreau and Albert Schweitzer have set a standard which cannot be ignored. Nevertheless, it is not easy to see or say just how the heroes of the future will live up to what is expected of them. Men today seem still to be in the throes of that identity crisis that ensued after the peak experience of humanism.

In times past the object of the quest was usually clear and definite. The hero set out to track and kill the prey, slay a monster, find a magical cauldron of rejuvenation (motif of supervitality), a golden fleece or a solar treasure. Then the quest turned inward for a while, taking love, intimacy and moral self-improvement as its aims. Eventually, it moved outward again, shifting toward the far horizons of territorial expansion and intellectual invention. Now, if the quest is once again concentrating inward, the question facing men may be, What am I, as hero, looking for within myself that I have never *yet* been able to find?

This question, or others like it, certainly seems to be on the minds of those many men today who have involved themselves, one way or another, in exploring 'men's issues' and re-evaluating the role of the hero, seen through his own eyes. In doing so, they often happen upon an insight that is generously supported by all the inherited lore: that is, the problematic relation, or lack of it, between the hero and his father. In almost no instance of classical or medieval hero-lore does the son of a hero amount to anything, and in most cases, as we have noted several times above, the hero does not even know who his father is. His bond to Woman, already clear from prehistoric times, continues to sustain the hero to the point where he recreates it through his surrender to the individual woman in the cult of *fin amors*; but then is he left with her as his sole surviving ally?

Perhaps the hero's lack of relationship to his father reflects the real-world situation in which the father embodies the value-system of patriarchy and male-dominance, fundamentally hostile to the heroic path. This certainly seems to be the issue dramatized in the great Russian novel, *Petersburg*, by Andrei Biely, where the young protagonist struggles with the temptation to become a terrorist and blow up his authoritarian father. A second masterpiece of modernism, *Ulysses*, by James Joyce, also explores the theme of the father-quest. Using the framework of the *Odyssey*, Joyce compresses the ten-year wanderings of the Homeric hero into the day-long jaunt around Dublin. The novel plays on the missing link between Ulysses and his son, Telemachus, who appears as the character Stephen Dedalus (called 'Stephen Hero' in the original draft of Joyce's earlier work, *Portrait of the Artist as a Young Man*). Young Stephen yearns to achieve an heroic destiny as an artist who can 'forge upon the smithy of my soul the uncreated conscience of my race', but he must do so without benefit of a fatherly model or paternal support, and for lack of this he suffers bitterly.

Whatever the success of current efforts to revalorize 'male bonding', the father-son bond is surely the most crucial and least understood. For men to claim their power and give the hero of the future a new direction they will have to deal with the casualties of this tragic omission: the raw and aching rebels, outcasts without a cause, the war-weary and sexually forsaken, men who love too tough, the battered boys and sons abandoned, all wounded by the father. For all of these, fate may rest in where they find their heroes, those they choose as father-figures whenever the genetic father is inadequate or missing. So much in the existing hero lore attests to maternal bonding as the source from which the hero draws his birthright and lifelong inspiration, but what he makes of this inspiration in the world at large depends upon the father-link, the self-shaping capacity. If his character stems primarily from the mother, he is lost. He regresses through Tristan and Jason to the pathetic lover-sons of the Great Goddess. Where he finds the father, by creative identification, not in the blood-line but in the flesh-and-blood lives of men who have excelled as warriors and lovers, inventors, explorers, athletes and poets – there lies the direction to which he might now be turning.

Wherever the way leads, man as the hero will always need a challenge to measure his power, a true and honourable test and a noble aim for his ever-evolving will. Until the hero finds himself again, coming through another advance and a fateful transfiguration, heroes will be found where they are needed, and more often than not, the true figure of the hero will be distorted and slandered, adapted to false ideologies and alien causes. Nevertheless, his survival skills are supreme. He will live on as he always has, larger than life yet vulnerable to its most delicate demands, dazzling and dangerous as beauty itself and, like beauty, captured and held as long as his moment lasts in the eye of the beholder.

Mastery of Brute Force

In all lands and all times, mastery of brute force has been the primary mark of the hero. Viewed along anthropological lines, this reveals the natural glorification of those powers of male aggression essential to the survival of the species. In a deeper sense, man is always implicated by the excess power he wields. Every contest between hero and monster suggests how the two must become entangled, psychologically, as surely as they were when engaged, eye to eye and limb to limb, in the throes of mortal conflict. (Antonio Pollaiuolo, *Hercules and the Hydra*, late 15th century)

Shamans, Beastmasters, Regents

From the age of *homo erectus*, around 750,000 BC, countless unnamed heroes must have arisen for humankind to have survived the perils of prehistory. No wonder, then, that the first myths recorded world-wide preserve the figure of the hero already raised to a god-like status. Typically represented in monumental style as a regent or god-king, as seen in the Assyrian bas-relief of Gilgamesh, he still retains the marks of the beastmaster, Lord of the Animals. Among the superhuman feats attributed to the hero is the shamanic control of nature, the placation of hostile elements such as storm and flood. Here the effigy of an Angolan tribal hero holds spirit-figures who represent intermediaries between the people and the forces of nature. Maui, a comparable deified hero of Polynesia, writhes with spiralling, surging currents of supervitality as he pulls the island of New Zealand up from the cosmic ocean. (Gilgamesh and the lion, Assyrian relief, 8th century BC; Chief of the Chokwe, Angola, 19th century; the god Maui, pulling the North Island of New Zealand, 1898)

Mayhem and Majesty of the Hunt

The difference between a somatic and a spiritual ethos is like the difference between blood and breath. In many archaic languages (Greek, Hindu, Hebrew, Egyptian), the word for 'breath' is the same as for 'spirit' in the sense of something unseen, incorporeal. But blood is a different kind of entity, more substantial and less controllable than breath. In combat with the prey, the pounding of the hero's blood must have reached thunderous intensity and the shedding of blood usually marked the outcome, one way or the other. Today, perhaps only a visit to a slaughterhouse would be gruesome enough to suggest the brutality of the primordial contest between man and beast, yet the savage, majestic beauty of such encounters cannot be denied, either. The reverence felt by the hero for the hunted was ultimately transferred into an ethical sense that dictated a controlled and respectful use of violent force – a sense of restraint tragically lacking in the modern world. (Gold plaque with repoussée decoration, from Ziwiye, Iran, 8th–7th century BC; Rubens, *Lion Hunt* (detail), 1617; George Catlin, *Buffalo Hunt* (detail), 1855)

Domestic Hunter, Male Icon, Phallic God

In his earliest natural habitat, *homo sapiens* was a humble domestic hero dedicated to hunting and protection of the hearth. Although procreation was not known to result from insemination by the male, he was celebrated for his phallic stature through the identification of the erection with blood, thunder, solar heat and the sun itself – analogies widely preserved in indigenous societies today (far left).

Only in very late times, when theological abstraction came into play as an effect of man's capacity to think himself out of this world, did the phallic hero assume the status of a dominating, patriarchal power, as suggested by the arrogant ('cocky') pose of the ithyphallic Shiva. (Father of the tribe, wooden figure from Nias, Indonesia; family in New South Wales, engraving, 1793; ithyphallic Shiva, India)

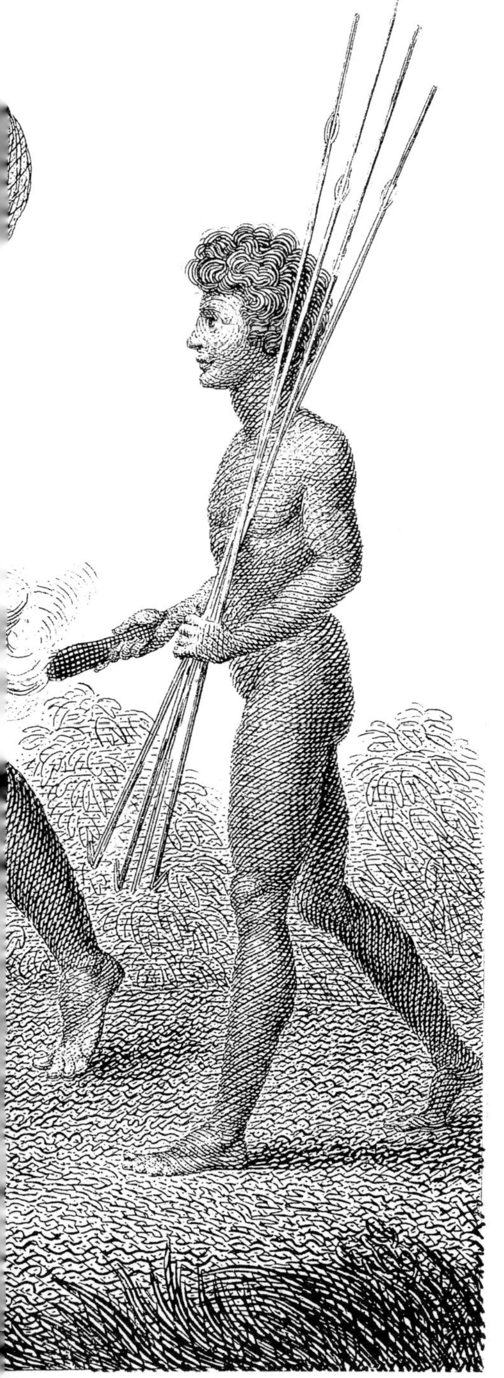

Woman, Dragon, Rescue

The image of the hero battling the dragon appears in many variations, reflecting different world-views and diverse ideologies. Represented in his deific aspect, the hero is often shown as a figure of celestial radiance, descending to earth to vanquish the dark terrestrial powers, or rescue an earthbound woman (below). On the vertical axis, heroic mythology easily fosters a specious division between heaven and hell, sky and earth, god and nature, man and woman; but the hero can never be fully disidentified from his natural origins. Although the gestures of combat are highly stylized, a Persian miniature of Rustam fighting a dragon (right) clearly places the hero and his adversary in the very bowels of the earth. The roiling texture of the landscape suggests in a vivid way how the dragon emerges from, and is identical with, the bowels of the earth, terrestrial counterpart to the human bowels, the guts, the seat of courage where the true metals of the hero are forged and tempered. (Frederick Leighton, *Perseus and Andromeda,* 1891; *Rustam and Rakhsh combatting a dragon,* Persian manuscript c.1585)

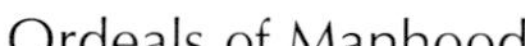

Ordeals of Manhood

On the heroic path man became so habituated to testing himself against overwhelming powers that when the necessity for such exertions was not forced upon him by nature, he resorted to inventing his own ordeals. Since his surfeit, his capacity to exceed himself, is not self-evident as it is in woman, man down the ages has affirmed it in the form of ritual ordeals, tests and initiations of manhood. Some of these were inconceivably gruesome, as Catlin's on-the-scene rendering of the Mandan Sundance Ordeal leaves no doubt (right). Physical stamina and mental concentration alike mark the hero who goes beyond the norm, like Mongaku Shonin beneath the waterfall (above). Often such ordeals, either collective or individual, contain an ethical or purificatory motive related to the archaic notion of compensation: wherever man has under-achieved, falling short of his true capacity, he can compensate for it by over-achieving in some agonistic feat. (*Mongaku Shonin doing penance under a waterfall*, Japanese print by Kunigoshi, 19th century; George Catlin, *The Cutting Scene*, 1832)

Martyr and Warrior Psychosis

On the path of the warrior, the hero developed freedom and autonomy as long as combat was single and direct, foe to foe, but in large-scale conflict he faced situations that arose from outside the scale of his individual powers of action. There then appear deviants from the pure hero who is never motivated by imperatives from beyond himself. For the Aztecs the godhead was a rigid dyad, Omeyocan, the principle of the split-world. This vertical ideology required constant war as a way to maintain the world-order. As the warriors below were slain others rained down from heaven to rush into battle seeking, not victory and survival, but a glorious end in *xochimiquiztli*, the 'flower death'.

Likewise, the Christian martyr draws some of his glory from the mystique of violence generated by the conflict between this world and a superior one. Dragged to his death in passive submission, Saint George knows his sacrifice will be rewarded in another world – a comfortable assurance which the authentic hero denies to himself. (Bernardo Martorell, *St George dragged to martyrdom*, 15th century; page from Nutall Codex, Mexico, 15th century)

P SCIPIONI

Heroic Nobility

Nobility is always of the blood, but not necessarily the inherited blood. Prototype of the nobleman who embodies the higher striving of the human race, the hero often had to be tested by facing the risk of death as well as the dire necessity of imposing it on others. His courage was tempered by direct intimacy with violence. Yet the noble character, revealed here in two profiles from different eras and cultures, betrays no trace of brutality or blood-lust. Scipio idealized expresses the pensive restraint of the Renaissance man who sees through violence toward a higher striving, for culture and creativity. The profile of an American Indian chief displays a steadfast, all-measuring honesty of the kind that perhaps can only arise in oral cultures where a man is truly as strong as his word. The hero carries human dignity for all those of us who cannot – and it shows. (Verrocchio (attrib), *Scipio*, 15th century; Raven Blanket, chief of the Nez Percé Indians, early 20th century)

Hero and Goddess

Throughout all cultures, the relationship between the hero and the Magna Mater, or Great Goddess, is both intimate and ambivalent. Originally the progeny of matricentric cultures, the hero is fundamentally dedicated to serve the goddess, as primitive man served woman with the protective force of his aggressivity. Setting tests for the hero to prove his superfluity of power, or even provoking him to free himself from immature forms of dependence on her, the goddess can appear as his adversary or

nemesis: Hera antagonizing Herakles, for instance.

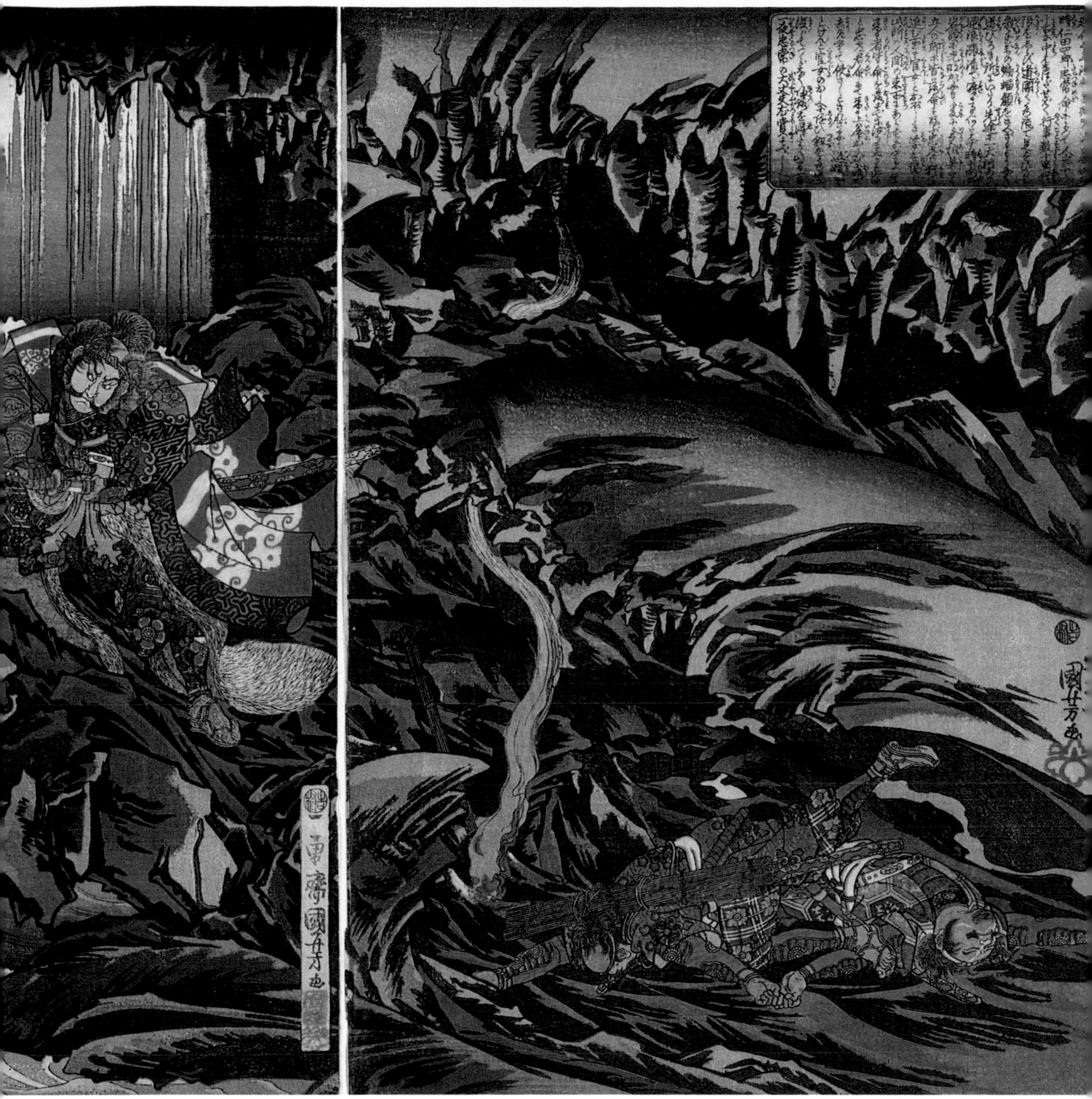

The Japanese hero, Tadatsune, stands in a forbidding landscape that suggests a terrain clawed into the raw and jagged ridges by a receding glacier. The Goddess appears in a cavern. Remains of the other heroes who have perished here lie heaped on the right. In an atmosphere saturated with violence there is a moment of tremendous pause. (*Tadatsune and the Goddess of Mount Fuji*, coloured print by Kuniyoshi, c.1844)

Male Bonding and the Dangers of Power Abuse

Male bonding originated in the hunt and so, obviously and inevitably, it has been associated with blood-shedding and blood-sharing down the ages. In the blood-oath men united their power, each one becoming an extension of the other, each willing to die in the place of the other. Male bonding appears to be a phenomenon that suffers when extrapolated into a too-large scale. The responsibility for excess force and the management of violence, still controllable when the individual remains accountable, are lost in the mass psychosis of military orders. (Nazi parade, mid 1930s; Jacques-Louis David, *The Oath of the Horatii*, 1785)

Authority and Revolution

Very early in historical times, man turned his heroic exertions toward mental feats and techniques of self-transcendence. The path of introversion permitted the hero to exceed himself, not merely by extending his capacities in the physical world, but by surpassing his physical limits toward extra-physical, mystical realms.

But the authority-figure, be it religious or political, ultimately promotes rules and regimes which become repressive and self-serving, subsequently overthrown by new heroes who arise as radicals and revolutionaries. Zapata's battle for agrarian reform was an heroic act against repression and denial of the realities of the earth. (*The sage Shukadeva instructing King Savikshit* (detail), Kishangarh School, c.1760; Diego Rivera, *Agrarian leader Zapata*, fresco, 1931)

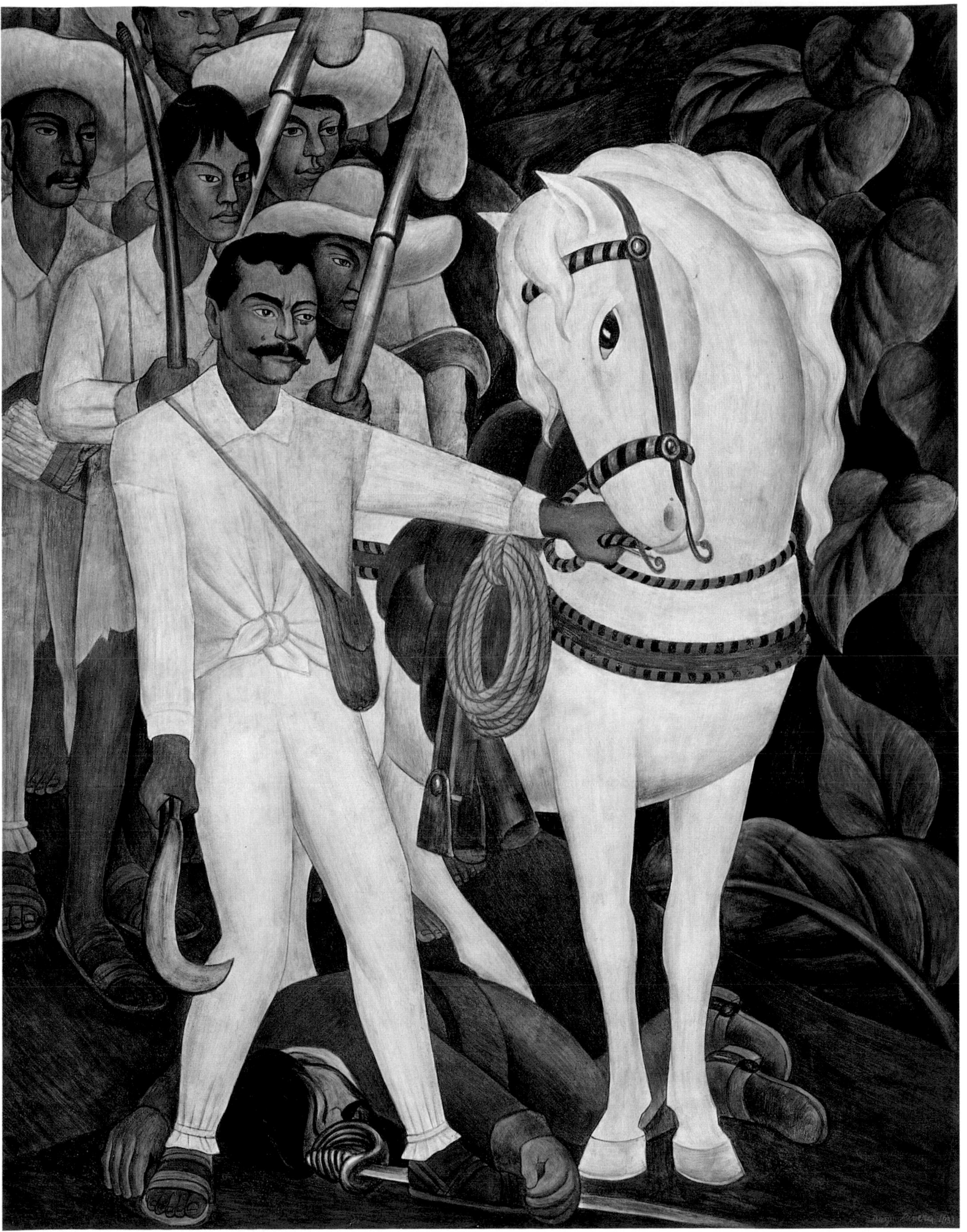

Ideologue and Unknown Hero

So many heroes have passed unknown, it is impossible to measure what humanity owes to those who have suffered and died to ensure it a future worth living. Thus, the entire world can respond to the sight of a lone anonymous student stopping a line of tanks, as if his defiance belonged to us all. But perhaps the heroic prowess is non-transferable. Next to the Chinese student, Lenin in his guise as ideological icon looks egregiously vain. Yet the hero of the people, depicted in this way, is capable of inspiring millions to do what apparently would be unthinkable or impossible for them on their own. Is there an uncanny power in the mere (empty) symbol of the hero, or is this power falsely conferred upon it by those who have never known an heroic moment in their lives? (V. Ivanov, poster of Lenin, 1967; a lone Chinese man facing tanks heading for Tiananmen Square, 1989)

Love and Sublimation

Throughout the Middle Ages the hero underwent a profound transformation reflected primarily in two aspects of European culture. Roving knights who once looked for adventures and more dragons to slay, thereby to revitalize themselves, now turned to the quest for spiritual redemption and atonement with the powers beyond: the quest for the Holy Grail.

The second trend, the shift toward romantic love and the idealization of woman, has also been interpreted as a path of sublimation, but its carnal aspect always remains highlighted in

the heroic lore of the times. The primordial triangle of hero-monster-woman is here converted into the triangle of lover-husband-wife. Tristan, the illicit lover of Isolde, betrothed to his uncle Mark, suffers not only the pangs of Eros before his lover's gaze, but also the mortal enmity of his rival, depicted by Mark's stabbing him with an arrow. (King Mark wounds Tristan, from the *Roman de Tristan*, early 15th century; Dante Gabriel Rossetti, *How Sir Galahad, Sir Bors and Sir Percival were fed with the Sanct Grael* (detail), 1864)

Facing the Unknown

The vastness of nature and the huge dimensions of the physical earth have always challenged man to heroic efforts. On land and sea, there have always been new frontiers to cross, uncharted realms to explore. Sometimes the hero faced the unknown in naked aloneness, or solely with an animal as his companion, such as the horse. In Redon's drawing, man and animal are shown as one in the gesture of recoiling before the unknown, yet in the same moment, gathering the strength to plunge into it.

Other times, men ventured together in small bands to face the raw elements. Bonded alike by courage and mutual fear, they experienced moments of intimacy which simply do not readily translate into words: you had to be there. In great measure,

man's sense of his own heroic potential lives within him incommunicably, as deep and silent as the depths of the sea. (Odilon Redon, *La Peur*, 1865; engraving, from Jules Verne, *Twenty Thousand Leagues under the Sea*)

Comfort in Death

Moments when men face death together can be private or intensely public, but the way men die, when they die heroically, remains intimate and inviolable. In antiquity, the most celebrated case of male grief for a lost comrade was that of Achilles, whose best friend Patroclus borrows his armour only to die in it. Heroic emotion shapes the *Iliad* because the heroes feel in excess of what they can explain or express, and the superfluity must be absorbed by those around them.

Other moments of facing death together are utterly apart and private, as with the samurai who helps a mortally wounded comrade to drink. The tender strength of his gesture draws us close to their bond – and the rest is silence. (Yoshitoshi, *A Samurai giving water to a wounded comrade*, 19th century; Gavin Hamilton, *Achilles lamenting the death of Patroclus* (detail), 1760–63)

The Duality of Violence

Whatever his guises or disguises, his transformations down the ages, the hero remains a part of ourselves we cannot afford to ignore. Saving the day time after time, he can neither be tamed nor repressed. At moments filled to excess with the violence that arises within himself, he alone is capable of meeting and mastering its counterpart, the violence from without: thus the duality perennially displayed in the form of the minotaur, half man, half bull.

In its more subtle aspects, heroic lore always reminds us of this precarious, agonistic situation in which the hero is interfused with the monstrous forces he seeks to overcome. The bull (without) is complemented by the snake (within), the fiery coiling power of Kundalini, the serpent power. Because he incorporates the potential for his own destruction man is truly monstrous – otherwise he could not be truly heroic. (Male figure encircled by a serpent, Melanesian, 19th century; Theseus kills the Minotaur, Greek vase-painting, 5th century BC)

Themes

Quest for Frontiers

Is the human being both a creature of earth and something more, or simply a creature of earth who strives for something more? All religious conceptions attribute to humanity a transcendent element called spirit or soul, but in the hero this extra something is purely indigenous. It might be said that what is spiritual in the hero is just the human spirit itself, taken to its extreme pitch of striving. How natural it is, then, for people at large to feel uplifted by the feat of the lonely warrior, the explorer, the poet or the athlete. Sherpa Tensing who stands atop Everest does not exemplify any religious or political creed. His final step to the top is not a 'giant leap for mankind': it is simply one man's step magnified in dimension by the aspiration of humankind, as a whole, toward what only the individual, only the hero, can achieve. (Sherpa Norgay Tensing on the summit of Mt Everest, 29 May, 1953)

quon nomme. pakamagan, Il blegne dans un

Sunmen and Phallic Cults

Religion in a formal sense did not exist in the culture of our paleoanthropic ancestors where the hero made his initial appearance as hunter and provider. Nevertheless, the attitude of the cave people was intensely religious, especially regarding their own bodily functions as related to the kingdoms of nature. The connection of solar heat with phallic and animal powers is eloquently demonstrated in petroglyphs of a hero figure with penis and tail holding up a solar labyrinth as if it were an outsize sporting trophy (right).

The long phase of our pre-religious experience has often been labelled as the era of 'solar-phallic' religions. These arose in matricentral cultures where phallic display was not taken as a measure of fathering power, but rather an epiphany of male excess, pure and simple. In archaic thinking, blood and thunder were analogues, so the solar god, prototype of the hero, often appears holding the phallic thunderbolt (below left).

Archaic traces of the hero's humble beginnings show a profound continuity, if one knows how to look for it: for instance, in the conventions used to represent early regents and law-givers. A cylinder-seal of the Persian King, Darius (upper left), is loaded with them: a deific winged double (solar god), arrows (sun-rays), lions being hunted (solar animals), chariot wheel (sun-circle). Here the phallic aspect is no longer blatantly evident, because Darius is a patriarchal progenitor, linked genetically to a lineage of kings. It remains however in full display in such archaic intruders from the backwoods (below right) as Robin Goodfellow. (Left: Darius hunting, Persian seal impression, c.500 BC; Samurai, from a folding screen, 19th century; Celtic bronze statuette from France, Roman period; Sioux Indian chief decorated with the sun and moon, c.1700. Right: wooden figure of war god from New Mexico; ithyphallic man holding sun disk, Bronze Age, Sweden; Robin Goodfellow, woodcut, early 17th century.)

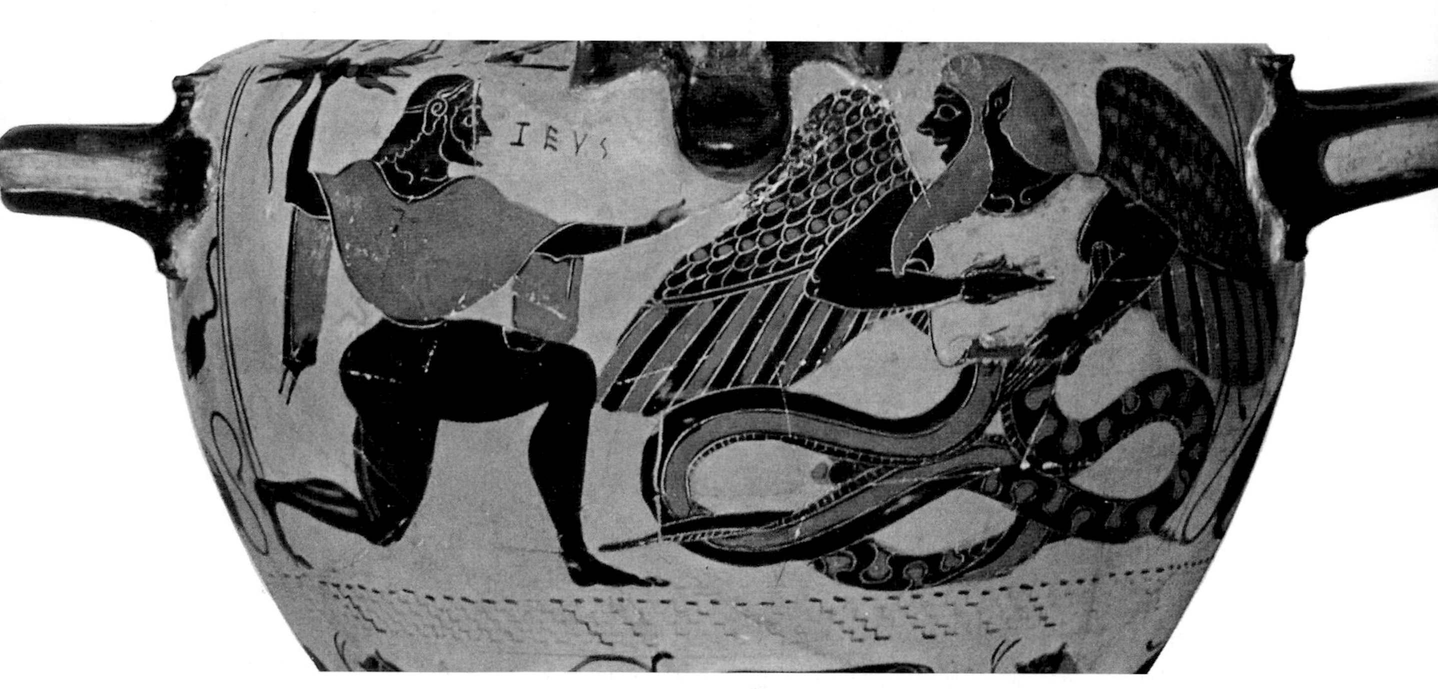

Serpent Power, Dragon Treasure

All forms of 'classical' mythology may be considered as polished scripts based on prehistoric scenarios carried in the racial memory, recording how the male risked blood and bowels to save the day. In a Greek vase painting of Zeus battling Typhon (opposite below), the streamlined form of the monster is easily seen as a schematic rendition of the human torso: lungs (wings) and bowels (entwined serpentine coils). Likewise, the monstrous face of Humbaba (far left) is a mute epiphany of the vulnerable, life-sustaining bowels.

Dragons are variously represented as single-headed or many-headed. In the human body, the serpent power is single in the writhing electrification of the spinal column, mastered in feats of yoga; yet it remains multiform and elusive as it surges in the bloodstream. Woman, who sheds blood openly and survives (indeed, even seems to be regenerated by the efflux), was herself identified with the serpentine adversary of the hero whenever patriarchal taboo figured in the script. For the same reason Typhon is given a female visage. (Top row: face of Humbaba, Babylonian terracotta, c.700–500 BC; Herakles wrestling Achelous, Greek vase, 5th century BC; *Hiawatha defeats the Kenabeek*, 19th century engraving. Bottom row: Zeus attacking Typhon, Greek vase, 6th century BC; Franz von Stuck: *Sensuality*, 1891.)

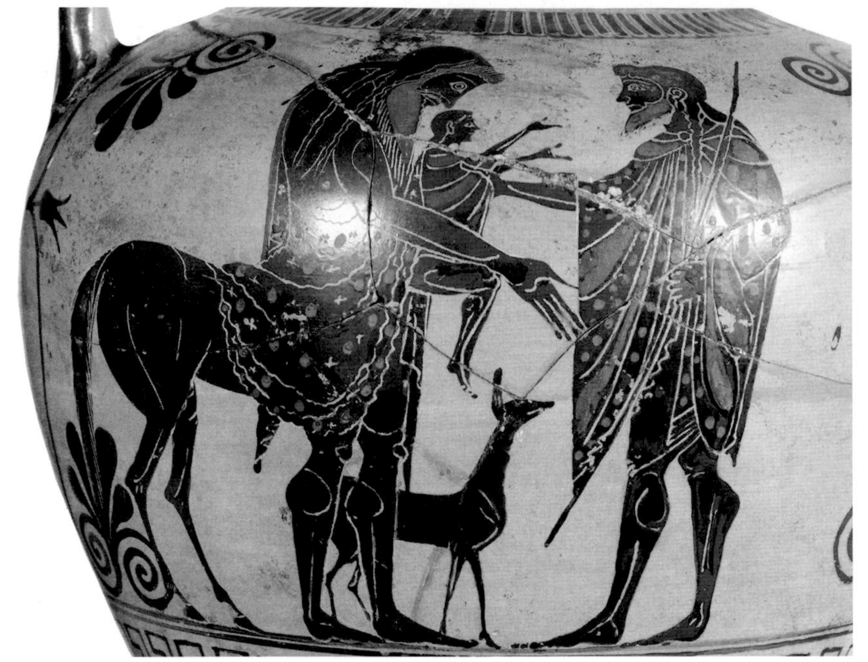

Initiation and Ordeal

When the hero was not being tested by the challenges nature itself thrust upon him, he sustained his stamina and upheld his capacity for male excess by means of initiations and ordeals, the rites of manhood. As these often consisted of ritualized versions of hunting and stalking techniques, their value was highly pragmatic as well. In this way the elders and battle-tried heroes passed on their survival skills to the next generation of men.

As heroic prowess always demands excess, ordeals of manhood often went to grotesque and tortuous extremes. Young men were required to perform physical acts of excruciating difficulty, or subject themselves to long ordeals of pain and deprivation. Whether or not the hero ever proved he could use his superfluous powers in other, equally demanding but non-contrived situations, his capacity to endure such trials was taken as full assurance of heroic self-mastery: curiously, the rehearsal of pain became more significant than the occasions where pain might actually be encountered. (Left: Peleus delivers Achilles to Chiron, Greek vase, 6th century BC; Australian aborigine being prepared for puberty rite, watercolour, 19th century. Below: Aboriginal drawing of Yurlunggur the snake as a huge womb with children. Right: human acrobats and feline leaping between horns, Yoruba mask, Nigeria; Sunnyasis performing feats of endurance over a fire, Madras, 1785; Sioux sun dance, 19th century.)

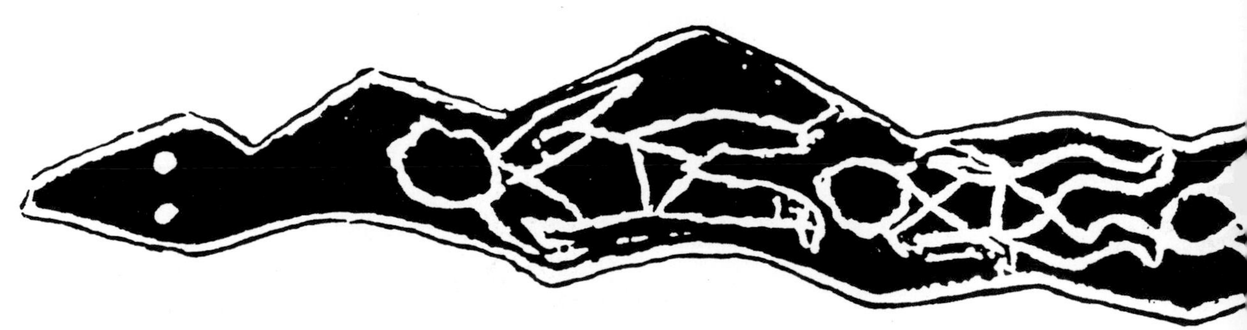

Herakles and the Royal Lion

Among the various animals associated with the hero and his prowess, the lion is prominent. It was the power animal of the Greek hero, Herakles, even though the lion so often represented in images of this hero (right, above and below) was unknown to the regions of Greece. This may suggest a prehistoric African origin for Heraklean myth and Mediterranean hero-lore in general. Today, Giele, a King of Dahomey, is still represented in full leonic epiphany (right).

Hand-to-hand combat with lions is difficult to imagine in modern times, and hardly necessary with the benefit of special effects that give us cinematic heroes battling the most extraordinary computer-driven monsters. Yes, but the life-force cannot be transmitted mechanically or electronically, no matter how sophisticated its simulations. The lion in all its variations represents the supreme feat of the hero in incorporating the life-force of the adversary – initially, the prey he pursued in the hunt, later the single foe he faced in mortal combat. Hero and lion pictured together in mortal conflict reveal this vital interfusion with a palpable impact, communicating a sense of physical peril no electronic spook can convey. (Top row: Giele, King of Dahomey, as a lion, painted wooden figure; constellation of Herakles fighting the serpent guarding the golden apples, woodcut, 1485; Herakles and the lion, Greek vase, 6th century BC. Bottom row: Sassanian king fighting lions, silver bowl, 4th century AD; Mithridates VI wearing lion's head, Greek, 1st century BC; Herakles and the Nemean Lion, Florentine bronze, early 16th century.)

The Wild Hunt

In the hunt man experienced a magical fraternity which perhaps underlies all later instances of 'male bonding'. In primitive society, heroic actions performed during the hunt were celebrated and commemorated in ritual and song, without any particular hero being singled out. In the great frieze from Çatal Hüyük (far left, top), no human figure stands above any of the others, while the prey, antlered and erectile, is presented in monumental scale.

Incorporation of the animal powers was one of humankind's first religious experiences, attested in ritual attire and markings, like those of the eagle dancer (far left), as well as in mimetic behaviour. The most powerful of all heroic encounters were those involving some form of traumatic sensation, such as the disembowelment of the prey, pictured in the famous scene at Lascaux (left, top). Long after such events were common, echoes of the wild hunt persisted as a post-traumatic stress reponse, typically imagined in the violent, riotous imagery of Odin and his band. (Top row: hunting scene from Çatal Hüyük, Turkey, Neolithic; cave painting at Lascaux, France, Paleolithic. Bottom row: young Australian aborigines miming animals in initiation rite, 19th century; Peter Nicolai Arbo: *The Wild Hunt of Odin* (detail), 1872. Far left: eagle dancer on inscribed shell from Spiro Mound, Oklahoma.)

Hero and Horse

In early pictoglyphs representing solar mythology, the horse is inscribed with spiral markings and dot-patterns which suggest a fine, far-seeing intelligence. Horse and hero are literally portrayed as one in the figure of the centaur, or in mimetic versions of artificial horsemen found in Greek vase painting. In all instances, a close collaboration between the human and equine intelligences is always implied. Persian art (below left) provides the unusual dramatic scene of a horse protecting his sleeping master from a lion. (Warrior wearing solar amulets leading horse, drawing from a Greek vase; solar decoration on the Trundholm horse, bronze, c.1300 BC; *Rahksh fighting a lion while Rustam sleeps*, from the Shāhnāmeh, 1486.)

One cowboy hero of the American West, the Lone Ranger, is always associated with his horse, Silver. Here modern TV lore reflects the age-old theme of the companionship between hero and horse. Unlike his identification with the lion, the hero's bond to his horse is not based on peril or adversarial power, although Alexander the Great had to tame Bucephalus in the same way that cowboys today still break their broncos. (Horse dancers from a Greek vase, 6th century BC; Alexander breaking in Bucephalus, bronze statuette, 4th–3rd century BC.)

Arms and the Man

Arma virumque cano: 'Arms and the man I sing.' So begins the *Aeneid* by Virgil. The celebrated armour of Achilles (left) was forged by Hephaistos and endowed with magical powers. The same idea is expressed in the legend of the grass-cutting sword of Prince Yamoto (below left), Japanese counterpart to King Arthur whose sword, Excalibur, was also an instrument of magic. Perhaps this mythologem anticipates our modern belief in the supernatural potency of technological weapons, instruments which have practically eclipsed the human-based powers of the hero.

For most of human history, the weapons man used in heroic combat remained remarkably stable: club, knife, spear, sword, bow and arrow. Engravings in the Valltorta Gorge (far left) show warriors in rigorous poses armed with bows and arrows and, possibly, spearthrowers. The same technology was still in use among native Americans (centre, top) at the dawn of the 20th century, but figures of that period contain the telling detail of a prairie rifle added to the stone age arsenal. Before explosive technology prevailed, the hero's survival depended upon his skill in handling weapons and negotiating the swift strategies of hand-to-hand combat. In the nuclear age, button-pushing does not require a lot of practice. (Far left: reconstruction of Palaeolithic painting with Valltorta Gorge, Spain. Centre: native American warriors; samurais in combat. Left: Hephaistos presents Thetis with armour for Achilles, Greek vase, 5th century BC; Kuniyoshi: *Prince Yamoto and his grass-cutting sword*, 1834–35.)

Minotauromachia

Among all the animals associated with the hero, the bull is perhaps the most enduringly complex and mysterious. The monstrous hybrid of a man with a bull's head, the minotaur (bottom), is a stirring image of masculine identity, replete with lust, violence and a dark, dauntless intention.

The bison figures prominently in prehistoric cave art celebrating the

hunt, as well as in the religious symbolism of the Hindus where Nandi, the mystical vehicle of Shiva, assumes a monumental presence (far left). In Nandi the hot, roiling masculinity of the bull appears to be tamed and safely contained, as would have been accomplished in the rigorous introversions of Indian yoga; but elsewhere the forces of the bull are rampant, as if the slaying of the Cretan Minotaur by Theseus has to be repeated over and over again by every man to keep the taurine excess in check. The lurid spectacle of the bullfight (below) attests to this recurrent need.

Heroic excess in service to violence so brutal it transgresses our sense of human limits seems to be the hidden menace of the bull: i.e., the genocidal potential of the male. In a poster announcing Buffalo Bill's Wild West Show (bottom), the icon of the impresario, imposed on the bull, presents us with a sudden, startling epiphany of the white man who came, indeed, and mindlessly slew the heroic races of indigenous people, hunting their sacred animal to near extinction solely for the profit of its tongue and hide.

(Opposite: Nandi, sculpture at Mysore, 1659; Herakles capturing the Cretan bull, Greek vase, 5th century BC; Magdalenian engraving on bone, Raymonden, France; Bronze Age petroglyphs at Kyrgyzstan; Theseus and the Minotaur, Greek vase, 6th century BC. Above: Goya, plate from *Tauromaquia*, 1815. Right: poster advertising Buffalo Bill, 1900.)

The Hero in Love

Of all the challenges facing the hero, his confrontation with love has certainly been the most influential in shaping the manners and mores of modern life. The great prehistoric shift from hunter to warrior brought us as a species into history, and the epochal shift from warrior to lover brought us into psychology. Certainly, early versions of god and goddess as lovers were common to both India and Greece, and often the god-figure, such as Shiva (centre right), exhibited proto-heroic traits; but the psychological complexities of personal love only emerged in Europe from the 8th century onward. The hero in conflict with his passions often lived in the exquisite flux between forced separation and immortal soul-fusion, thus defining the core polarity of Romantic Love.

Gradually, love altered the hero's aggressive traits into moral qualities. In a painting of blatant phallic allegory, Botticelli pictured the change as the emasculation of Mars by Venus (below right), where the lance of the exhausted hero becomes a mere plaything for putti. Although giving up his former powers, the hero is always assured of getting the girl in the end. (Miniature from the *Minnesinger* manuscript, c.1300; *Shiva and Parvati*, 1780–90; Botticelli, *Mars and Venus*, c.1485. Far right: Edward Burne-Jones, *Sigurd*, 1862; *The Victor's Prize*, lithograph, 1905.)

The Hero Facing Death

In all cultures and traditions, the hero is defined by how he faces death. We shall all die, not certain of when or how, perhaps even of why, but we prefer not to think about that. The hero reminds us of the immutability of death and raises in us the courage to accept it and go forward, while still living, to meet it openly and unconditionally.

Cults of the hero, especially prominent in the Hellenic world, seem to have promoted the notion that through death the hero leaves a measure of his life-force unspent. More than a model act, the death is proof that something indestructible lives in the human breast. It may be in death more than life that the hero is able to transmit his male surfeit to others, as Socrates certainly did for succeeding generations, down to our time.

(*Martyrdom of St Thomas Becket*, manuscript illumination, c.1200; titlepage of a life of Davy Crockett, 1852.)

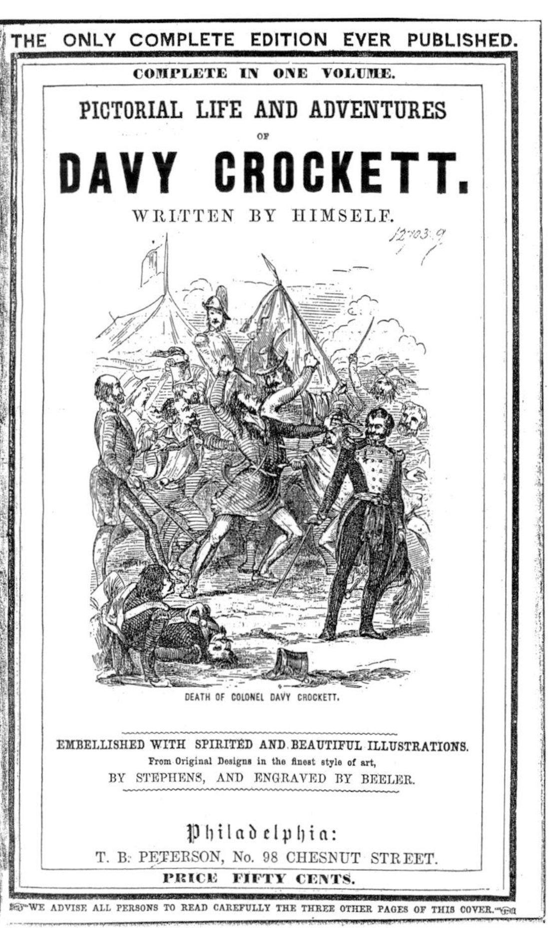

THE ONLY COMPLETE EDITION EVER PUBLISHED.

COMPLETE IN ONE VOLUME.

PICTORIAL LIFE AND ADVENTURES

OF

DAVY CROCKETT.

WRITTEN BY HIMSELF.

DEATH OF COLONEL DAVY CROCKETT.

EMBELLISHED WITH SPIRITED AND BEAUTIFUL ILLUSTRATIONS.

From Original Designs in the finest style of art,

BY STEPHENS, AND ENGRAVED BY BEELER.

Philadelphia:

T. B. PETERSON, No. 98 CHESNUT STREET.

PRICE FIFTY CENTS.

WE ADVISE ALL PERSONS TO READ CAREFULLY THE THREE OTHER PAGES OF THIS COVER.

Nevertheless, what makes a man's death truly heroic is not ultimately the consequences or benefits it has for others, great as these may be. Rather, it is the uncompromising style that turns the surrender to death, due from us all, into one man's act of pure autonomy. This is variously illustrated in famous death-scenes, from Thomas Becket to Davy Crockett.

Socrates's death was quasi-suicidal: condemned to die, he voluntarily drank poison. The act of taking one's own life has often been considered as the mark, if not the requisite, of the hero. With Homeric heroes and Japanese samurai alike, it was a way of preserving honour – in the heroic code, a value more to be prized than life itself. (Samurai committing hara-kiri, by Yoshitoshi; Jacques-Louis David, *The Death of Socrates*, 1787; Gaul committing suicide after killing his wife, Roman copy of Greek sculpture, c.220 BC.)

Woman as Hero

The heroine is not simply a female hero, and she deserves a full treatment in her own right, distinct from her male counterpart. In some notable cases, however, woman has appeared in the role of the hero, acting in a manner barely distinguishable from a man. These are the special instances of masculinized women, such as Camilla in the *Aeneid* (below centre). Her appearance and actions, recounted in

several hundred lines of vivid poetry, make her the full equal of the male warriors on the scene. All in all, she might as well be a man.

Feminine hero-figures are prominent in Germanic lore where the Valkyries command a terrific presence on the battle-field (below right). In folk-lore these women are associated with the Wild Hunt of Odin and, sometimes, they are portrayed as ferocious hostesses welcoming departed warriors into the otherworld. There seems to be nothing in their feminine make-up which in any way compromises their power or prevents them from being a formidable match for any man. The same applies for Rosie the Riveter, an iconic hero-woman of World War II (below left).

Joan of Arc, certainly the most famous of hero-women (left), is noted for two distinct feminine traits: her virginity and her susceptibility to 'intuition' in the form of mystical voices. These features of the 'fair sex' only make her heroic prowess seem all the more spectacular. (*Joan of Arc receiving the sword Fierbois*, 1656; *Rosie the Riveter*, American World War II poster; *Camilla fighting*, illustration to the *Aeneid* by Carlotta Patrina, 1944; Peter Nicolai Arbo, *Valkyries*, 1869.)

Ancestral and National Heroes

Every nation and race has its indigenous heroes, many of which continued to be celebrated down into modern times. In the framework of *Völkerpsychologie*, it has been common to attribute the character of a people, say the Russian Slavs, to the person and actions of their leading hero: in their case, Ilya Muryamets (far right). This notion clearly expresses the basic assumption of heroic descent by affirming a moral and characterological descent, rather than a genetic one.

The famous image of Aeneas carrying his father, Anchises, away from the ruins of Troy on his shoulders (left), exemplifies the same belief, for Aeneas becomes the progenitor of the Romans even though he is not of their racial stock. Likewise, T. E. Lawrence (below right), the hero who deeply influenced the formation of a modern identity among the Arab nations, was British.

The associations linking a hero to his destined people may be historical, as we find with Vercingetorix, the Gaulish hero whose exploits at the time of Julius Caesar are firmly recorded (right). Or it may be purely mystical, as expressed in the image of Radigast (below left), an ethnogenic hero of the Slavs, pictured with an array of heroic token images: lightning, eagle, bull, horse, double-axe; and Hiawatha (below right), a legendary Native American hero celebrated by the poet, H. W. Longfellow. (Left: *Aeneas carrying his father from Troy*, a children's book illustration, 1828; Radigast, book illustration, 1918. Right: François Ehrmann, *Vercingetorix* (detail), 19th century. I. Bilibin, *Ilya Muryamets on his flying horse*, c.1900; T. E. Lawrence, photo; Frederic Remington, *Hiawatha fishing*, 1891.)

War Heroes through the Ages

In his famous study of the hero, Lord Raglan supported his argument that heroic lore arises from ritual and dramatic origins with the observation that epics and legends alike describe the hero as acting alone, often in a contrived or symbolically arranged setting. The ritual aspect of the hero's life in war is evident in the elaborate headgear and body-trappings of Indian braves in the West.

Until the era of fabricated national epics such as *El Cid*, the hero is never shown in the role of a military commander leading a group of men. It requires creative rescripting for a messianic figure such as Christ to be presented as a hero and placed at the head of a crusading army (far right). Before there was war there was the lone warrior, who may have plunged into battle naked, as the Picts and Celts were said to have done (below right). In our own time, one of the most memorable heroes was in fact an anti-war hero, an advocate of non-violent revolution. Gandhi's ethical individualism always stands by itself (below far right), distinct in value from the huge political changes he effected. (Top row: *Horatius holds the bridge*, engraving, 1818; *Christ leading the Crusaders*, English miniature, 14th century. Bottom row: Pict warrior, by John White, c.1585; Aztec warrior with eagle's hood, terracotta, c.1480. Far right: George Catlin, *Little Wolf*, 1845; Gandhi, photo, 1931.)

The Hero Facing Adversity

Challenged by the overwhelming forces of nature to discover, develop and apply his male excess of power, the hero faced countless risks posed by natural obstacles and the fury of the extremes, heat and cold. Sometimes the new worlds he opened resembled nothing others had seen before, like the snowbanks of the Polar Sea. Often he led others into the wilderness or across deserts, blazing the way across new frontiers. Pioneers of geographic expansion are heroes whose deeds are sure to affect the lives of many generations.

Exploring the unknown, there were incessant dangers, accidents and risks, so he was often pressed into the role of rescuer as well, sometimes requiring him to risk his life for others. Only by lending to others his excess of power was the survival of the group ultimately assured.

The most widely found mythological precedent for the hero's action of facing adversity appears in the hell-theme, the descent into the Underworld. This was a quest for hidden treasures, secrets of power and knowledge, or lost souls. Undoubtedly, the theme here reflects the actual experience of journeys undertaken in 'altered states' by shamans. His departure ceremonially attended by a Valkyrie, Odin on his eight-legged horse descends into hell where dead warriors are gathered in an underworld boat. Viking burials which sent the dead hero to sea in a burning boat were probably conceived in imitation of this potent motif. (Picture stone from Tjänjride, Sweden, showing Odin on his eight-legged horse, 9th century; Winslow Homer, *The Life-line*, 1884; boats in the ice, an engraving of 1825; George Caleb Bingham, *Daniel Boone escorting settlers through the Cumberland Gap* (detail), 1851–1852.)

The challenges and achievements of the hero are so diverse, it is no wonder that his temptations are equally so. These are the risks he must overcome, not simply to get to the next step of his chosen path or ordeal, but to keep himself on the path in the first place. Often enough, woman figures in the temptations because in mythic and psychological terms she represents the threat of being overcome by interiority, wherefrom he draws his excess of powers.

Sirens who lure Odysseus (top) and water-nymphs who seduce the young Argonaut Hylas (above) were popular temptation themes in antiquity. In the case of Jason (above right) the situation is changed by his accepting the magical and sexual assistance of the great sorceress, Medea – an extremely rare instance of classical power-sharing.

Dr Faustus (top right) represents the hero's risk of giving himself over to the prime temptations of power, knowledge and immortality. Goethe's version tells how he does in fact succumb to these temptations only to achieve redemption in the end, through returning to the realm of the Mothers. In the figure of Don Quixote (right), Cervantes presented a satire of late medieval chivalry when the 'knight

Temptations of the Hero

in shining armour' was already a stereotype and the fantasy of heroic adventure had become more appealing than the real thing. (Odysseus and the Sirens, Greek vase, 490 BC; John William Waterhouse, *Hylas and the Nymphs*, 1897; Gustave Moreau, *Jason and Medea*, 1865; Rembrandt, *Dr. Faustus*, etching, c.1652; *Don Quixote and Sancho Panza*, 19th century illustration.)

Further Reading

Alexander, Hartley Burr, *The World's Rim*, Lincoln, Nebraska, 1953
Bataille, Georges, *Erotism*, San Francisco, 1986
Benoist, Alain de, *Comment Peut-On Etre Paien?*, Paris, 1981
Bleibtreu, John, *The Parable of the Beast*, New York, 1968
Branston, Bryan, *The Lost Gods of England*, London, 1984
Brundage, Burr Cartwright, *The Fifth Sun*, Austin, Texas, 1983
Campbell, Joseph, *Creative Mythology*, New York 1968
Primitive Mythology, New York, 1976
The Hero with a Thousand Faces, New York, 1956
Carlyle, Thomas, *On Heroes, Hero-Worship and the Heroic in History*, London, 1841
Cassirer, Ernst, *The Myth of the State*, New Haven, Conn., 1946
Danielou, Alain, *Shiva and Dionysos*, New York, 1984
Eliade, Mircea, *A History of Religious Ideas*, 3 vols., Chicago, 1976–1985
Rites and Symbols of Initiation, New York, 1958
Evola, Julius, *The Metaphysics of Sex*, New York, 1983
Feldman, R., and Richardson, R.D., *The Rise of Modern Mythology*, London, 1972
Fontenrose, Joseph, *Python*, Berkeley, Calif., 1980
The Freud/Jung Letters, ed. William McGuire, Cambridge, Mass., 1968
Fromm, Erich, *The Anatomy of Human Destructiveness*, London, 1973
Getty, Adele, *Goddess*, London, 1990
Girard, René, *Violence and the Sacred*, tr. P. Gregory, Baltimore and London, 1977
Green, Miranda, *The Sun-Gods of Ancient Europe*, London, 1991
Highet, Gilbert, *The Classical Tradition*, New York, 1957
Huxley, Francis, *The Way of the Sacred*, Garden City, N.J., 1974
Jackson, W.T.H., *The Literature of the Middle Ages*, New York, 1960
Kaufmann, Walter, *From Shakespeare to Existentialism*, Princeton, N.J., 1959
Critique of Religion and Philosophy, Princeton, N.J., 1958
Tragedy and Philosophy, Princeton, N.J., 1968
Kerenyi, Carl, *The Heroes of the Greeks*, London, 1959
Leon-Portilla, Miguel, *Aztec Thought and Culture*, Norman, Oklahoma, 1963
McCracken, Harold, *George Catlin and the Old Frontier*, New York, 1959
Napier, E. David, *Masks, Transformation and Paradox*, Berkeley, 1986
Nelli, Reni, *L'Erotique des Troubadours*, Toulouse, 1963
Petit, Karl, *La Ducasse de Mons*, Mons, Belgium, 1984
Lord Raglan, *The Hero*, London, 1936
Rank, Otto, *The Myth of the Birth of the Hero*, New York, 1959
Regnier-Bohler, Danielle, ed., *La Legende Arthurienne*, Paris, 1989
Reich, Wilhelm, *The Mass Psychology of Fascism*, New York, 1980
Settegast, Mary, *Plato Prehistorian*, Cambridge, Mass., 1987
Seznec, Jean, *The Survival of the Pagan Gods*, New York, 1953
Silver, Alan, *The Samurai Film*, Woodstock, NY, 1983
Spence, Lewis, *An Introduction to Mythology*, London, 1921
Hero-Tales and Legends of the Rhine, London, 1915
Taylor, Gordon Rattray, *Sex in History*, London, 1953
Taylor, Lonn, and Marr, Ingrid, *The American Cowboy*, Washington, D.C. 1983
Turnbull, Stephen, *The Book of the Samurai*, New York, 1982
Wind, Edgar, *Pagan Mysteries in the Renaissance*, London and New York, 1968

Acknowledgments

Illustrations are acknowledged to the following collections and photographers with the following abbreviations: a above, b below, c centre, l left, r right:

Walters Art Gallery, **Baltimore** 70*a*; **Basle** Museum 6; Ross-Coomaraswamy Collection. Courtesy, Museum of Fine Arts, **Boston** 83*a*; **Cambridge** Museum of Archeology and Anthropology, Haddon Library Collection 70*c*, 74*b*; **Cincinnati** Art Museum, Ohio 36*a*; Musée Bargoin, **Clermont-Ferrand** 89*al*; Nationalmuseet, **Copenhagen** 13; From the Collection of Merlin & Mary Ann **Dailey**, Victor, New York, USA 48–9; Harmsen Collection, **Denver**. Photo Courtesy Amon Carter Museum, Fort Worth, Texas 43; Photo C.M. **Dixon** 39; National Gallery of Scotland, **Edinburgh** 61; **Florence**, Galleria degli Uffizi (Photo Scala) 33; Museo Archeologico (Photo Alinari) 77*b*; Hamburgisches Museum für Völkerkunde, **Hamburg** 35*r*, 62; Universitätsbibliothek, **Heidelberg** 82*a*; **Hosokawa** Collection, Japan 66*ar*; The University of **Iowa** Museum of Art, The Stanley Collection 35*l*; Topkapi Saray Museum, **Istanbul** 23; **London**, Associated Press 55; British Library 7, 23, 76*b*, 84*a*, 91*a*; British Museum 4, 66*al*, 68*al*, 68*ar*, 71*l*, 72*b*, 80*b*, 90*b*, 94*a*, 95*ar*; Werner Forman Archive 38*l*; The Hulton Deutsch Collection 51; Imperial War Museum 89*bl*; Reproduced by courtesy of the Trustees, The National Gallery 24, 29, 82–3*b*; © Royal Geographical Society 64; Tate Gallery 57; Courtesy of the Trustees of the Victoria and Albert Museum 71*ar*, 73*br*, 52; © **Manchester** City Art Galleries 94*b*; Board of the Trustees of the National Museums and Galleries on **Merseyside** (Walker Art Gallery) 40; Templo Mayor Museum, **Mexico** City (Photo Michel Zabe) 91*bl*; **Munich**, Alte Pinakothek 36*b*; Staatliche Antikensammlungen 68*b*; **New York**, Courtesy of the American Museum of Natural History 37; Brooklyn Museum 67*l*; Metropolitan Museum of Art, New York. Catherine Lorillard Wolfe Fund, 1931. All rights reserved, The Metropolitan Museum of Art 84–5*b*; Photograph courtesy of the Museum of the American Indian, Heye Foundation, 74*cl*; The Museum of Modern Art, New York. Abby Aldrich Rockefeller Fund. Photograph © 1995 The Museum of Modern Art, New York 53; Nasjonalgalleriet, **Oslo** 75*b*, 87*r*; **Paris**, Musée de l'Homme 72*a*; Musée du Louvre 50, (© Photo R.M.N.) 73*a*, 73*cl*, 34, 44, 46; Palais du Luxembourg 95*l*; **Philadelphia** Museum of Art 93*a*; **Private** Collection 42, 69*b*, 79*b*; Museo Nazionale, **Rome** (Photo Hirmer) 85*br*; Vatican Museums 63; **St Germain-en-Laye**, Musée des Antiquités Nationales 66*bl*; Washington University Gallery of Art, **Saint-Louis** 93*b*; ATA **Stockholm** 92; Riksantikvarieambetet, **Stockholm** 67*ar*; Thomas Gilcrease Institute, **Tulsa** 66*br*; Österreichisches Nationalbibliothek, **Vienna** 56; **United States** Air Force Collection 8; United States National Museum, on deposit with the National Collection of Fine Arts, Smithsonian Institution, **Washington** 91*ar*; The Royal Collection, **Windsor** © 1994 Her Majesty Queen Elizabeth II 41

Illustrations also reproduced from the following publications:

H. B. Alexander, *Mythology of all Races. North America* (1916) 71*br*; J. Chapelain, *La Pucelle, ou la France delivrée* (1656) 86*al*; E.S. Curtis, *The North American Indian* (1907–30) 47; C. Flammarion, *Les Étoiles et les Curiosités du Ciel* (1882) 72c; J. Franklin, *Narrative of a Second Journey to the Shore of the Polar Sea* (1825–27) 93c; *Good Words* (1862) 83*ar*; J. Hunter, *An Historical Journal of the Transactions at Port Jackson* (1793) 38; G.L. Jerrers, *Universal History for Children* (1828) 88a; H. Longfellow, *The Song of Hiawatha* (1891) 89*br*; J. Machal, *Mythology of All Races. Slavic* (1918) 88*b*; C. Alexander Marshack, *The Roots of Civilization* (1991) 80*ar*; B. Pinelli, *Istoria Romana* (1818) 90a; N. Tinbergen, *A Study of Instinct* (1951) 9; Virgil, *Aeneid*, (1944) 86*b*; Yoshitoshi, *Kwaidai Hyaku Senso* 60